American Justice 2014

American Justice 2014

Nine Clashing Visions on the Supreme Court

Garrett Epps

PENN

UNIVERSITY OF PENNSYLVANIA PRESS

PHILADELPHIA

Published by
University of Pennsylvania Press
Philadelphia, Pennsylvania 19104-4112
www.upenn.edu/pennpress

Printed in the United States of America

A Cataloging-in-Publication record is
available from the Library of Congress

Cover design by John Hubbard

ISBN 978-0-8122-4718-3 hardcover
ISBN 978-0-8122-9130-8 ebook

For Kathy
Mine ear is much enamour'd of thy note;
So is mine eye enthralled to thy shape.

This much I think I do know—that a society so riven that the spirit of moderation is gone, no court *can* save; that a society where that spirit flourishes, no court *need* save; that in a society which evades its responsibility by thrusting upon the courts the nurture of that spirit, that spirit in the end will perish.

—Learned Hand

Contents

Preface   1

Introduction: The Branch That Works   9

1. Balls and Strikes: Chief Justice John Roberts—
McCutcheon v. Federal Election Commission   21

2. Justice of Hearts: Justice Sonia Sotomayor—
*Dissenting, Schuette v. Coalition to Defend
Affirmative Action by Any Means Necessary*   35

3. Empathy for the Devil: Justice Antonin Scalia—
Dissenting, Windsor v. United States (Redux)   49

4. Enter Laughing: Justice Elena Kagan—
Dissenting, Town of Greece v. Galloway   61

5. Big Brother: Justice Anthony Kennedy—*Hall v. Florida*   73

6. In a Different Voice: Justice Clarence Thomas—
Susan B. Anthony List v. Driehaus   85

7. Bringer of Chaos: Justice Stephen Breyer—
National Labor Relations Board v. Noel Canning   97

8. The Alito Court: Justice Samuel Alito—
Harris v. Quinn   109

9. No Exit: Justice Ruth Bader Ginsburg—
Dissenting, Burwell v. Hobby Lobby Stores   123

Contents

Epilogue: Justice in Red and Blue   139

Appendix A: A Brief Guide to
Supreme Court Procedure   149

Appendix B: Biographies of
Current Justices of the Supreme Court   161

Appendix C: Major OT13 Cases
Discussed in This Book   171

Further Reading   175

Preface

In many ways, the US Supreme Court is as determinedly opaque as the National Security Agency. Though it maintains a talented public-information staff, the institution itself takes no responsibility whatsoever for explaining itself to the public. The product of the court's work—its oral argument transcripts, opinions, and orders—is made available promptly. The real work of the justices, however—deciding which cases to accept, discussing who should win cases and why, picking justices to write opinions, and criticizing the successive drafts—takes place behind a veil of secrecy that, for most of the court staff and law clerks, would be professional death to pierce.

Years after a justice dies, papers in a library may show how and why the court decided some issue. Historians revel in these sources, but for lawyers and citizens who must live today, they provide little help for understanding what the court is up to.

The court's secrecy is only part of the reason it is ill understood. A nine-member body has no "intention" the way an individual has. Thus the Supreme Court may not really "know" why it is doing what it is doing. Each decision is the sum of many calculations by lawyers, lower courts, and justices to shape issues in a certain way that produces a result. In time, this result may come to seem inevitable, but it almost certainly was not from the outset of the issue. (Think of the court's iconic school desegregation decision in *Brown v. Board of Education*. History shows us a bitterly divided court grappling with the issue—until a unanimous opinion improbably emerged.) Wherever the justices may think they are going, the court is quite likely to end up somewhere else, blown off course by the winds of judicial politics. "It is quite true what philosophy says; that life must be understood backwards," the philosopher Sören Kierkegaard wrote in 1843. "But then one forgets the other principle: that it must be lived forwards."

In the pages that follow, I have tried to give my sense of one year in the life of the Supreme Court—the "October 2013 term"—that began on the first Monday in October 2013 and (formally) ran until the day before the first Monday in 2014. In reality, OT13, as court watchers call it, reached its climax on the last day of June 2014, when the court delivered its final opinions in argued cases and adjourned.

During the months between the first full conference of late September 2013 and the dramatic announcement of opinions in *Burwell v. Hobby Lobby* and *Harris v. Quinn* on June 30, the court heard arguments in seventy-two cases and issued opinions in seventy of them. (Two were "dismissed as improvidently granted," or DIGed.) It also decided whether to hear some 7,500 cases submitted by petition for certiorari. Its opinions ranged from interpreting areas of the Constitution seldom before interpreted (e.g., when is the Senate in "recess" for purposes of presidential "recess appointment"?) to resolving mundane questions of statutory interpretation (e.g., do individual retirement accounts meet the statutory definition of "retirement funds" under the federal bankruptcy code?). Each opinion takes the court further into a legal future it cannot foresee. OT13, like every term, is a way station. Not for a generation, perhaps, will we know where the trail was leading. So view what you are about to read as a kind of traveler's diary. It makes no pretense to prophecy. I don't know where this court is going.

My role as a court watcher is unusual. Though I am accredited to the court's press gallery, my professional identity is as professor of law at the University of Baltimore. For twenty years, at five major law schools, I have studied and taught the court's constitutional jurisprudence. In my reporting, I look for the legal sources of the court's latest constitutional decisions; in my writing, I assess the court's work frankly and without any of the reticence that beat reporting sometimes imposes. I am not at the court to be a dispassionate observer. I write what I think. Sometimes what the court does delights me—not necessarily because it is what I would have decided myself but because I think it is conscientious, careful judging that shows respect for history and precedent; at other times, when the court majority seems slapdash, petty, and partisan, I feel like Evelyn Waugh reading the poet Stephen Spender: "to see him fumbling with our rich and delicate language is to experience all the horror of seeing a Sevres vase in the hands of a chimpanzee."

At the opening of OT13, I was sixty-three years old. I grew up in the white middle class of the twentieth-century South. Until I was fifteen years old, I lived under segregation—a regime of white supremacy enforced by legal coercion and extralegal violence. During the 1960s, as if in a dream, I witnessed the collapse of this icy monolith and the birth of a new and freer order.

That change occurred, in large part, because a generation of Americans decided—some eagerly, others with reluctance and dread—to bring to life the phrases "due process" and "equal protection" written into the Constitution in 1868. Contrary to popular myth, the Supreme Court did not liberate the South. Freedom came because of the bravery of the civil rights movement and the persistence of a bipartisan coalition in Congress. But the court played an important part.

Since that time, I have felt a kind of reverence for the Constitution and for the judges who follow it. That reverence led me after a career in journalism to law school and a second career following the Constitution and the court. I feel elation when courts and citizens read the document as a charter of equality and a set of rules for self-government. I feel anger and despair when they read it as a bulwark of privilege and paralysis.

I explain this only so that the reader will understand two things about *American Justice 2014*. First, of the court's published opinions, I have concentrated on those that interpret the Constitution because I know a little bit about the subject. I have almost nothing to say about employee stock ownership plans under the Employee Retirement Income Security Act or about the Copyright Act of 1978 as applied to the individual remote-antenna technology pioneered by Aereo Inc. This book assesses how the court cared for the Constitution during OT13 and refers to other cases if at all simply to illuminate ongoing constitutional disputes. I give short shrift even to some constitutional decisions when they did not represent important divisions within the court.

Second, what follows is my frank assessment of the decisions I discuss and of each of the nine justices as I observe them, watching them on the bench and reading reams of their writing. Not to hide the ball, I believe the court reached essentially the right decision in *Hall v. Florida* (procedures for assessing potentially intellectually disabled defendants in capital proceedings), *Susan B. Anthony List v. Driehaus* (organizations' right to challenge laws against making "false statements" during election campaigns), and *National Labor Relations Board v. Noel Canning* (use of "recess appointments" to name members of the National Labor Relations Board while the Senate was holding pro forma sessions). I believe the court erred, in some cases badly, in *McCutcheon v. Federal Election Commission* (aggregate limits on federal campaign contributions by individuals), *Town of Greece v. Galloway* (explicitly Christian prayer at town council meetings), *Schuette v. Coalition to Preserve Affirmative Action by Any Means Necessary* (statewide referendum on affirmative action in higher education admissions), *Harris v. Quinn* ("agency fees" for state-paid home health-care workers), and *Burwell v. Hobby Lobby Stores* (religious objections to insurance coverage for contraception as required by the Affordable Care Act).

You may very well disagree with me on any or all of these cases, but read on: if this book brings any pleasure and profit, it likely arises from whatever disagreement it stirs in the reader. With each passing year, as I learn more about the Constitution, I grow more convinced that the

Constitution of 2014—the 1789 text and the twenty-seven amendments that "we the people" have added during two centuries of blood and hardship—serves its function not when it provides answers but when it sparks questions. Some interpreters of the Constitution claim to understand and follow the "original understanding" of its authors; others insist they are applying a "living document" as history changes the meaning of its words. Others disclaim what Judge J. Harvie Wilkinson III of the Fourth Circuit called "cosmic constitutional theory," suggesting that judges should work with whatever lawyers' tools seem most suited to resolve a particular dispute. In the end, these methodological quarrels don't mean much to citizens. Whenever we debate the Constitution, we are in fact arguing not about words or history or legal precedent but about what our country should look like tomorrow. Our deepest desires for our country are often at odds with those of our neighbor; arguing about the Constitution gives us an alternative to settling our disputes by shedding blood.

As a peace-keeping device, the Constitution has a mixed record. Its original version failed catastrophically in 1861, producing a grisly national festival of fratricide. But since the Constitution was born again in 1865–70, it has succeeded well at providing us a set of rules for social argument and debate. It is, in effect, the deck of cards in our national high-stakes poker game. Those who read the cards differently than I do are welcome to do so. Walt Whitman, our great constitutional poet, once wrote of human identity that "every atom belonging to me as good belongs to you." Nowhere is that more true than of the Constitution and of its judicial vestals, the nine justices of the US Supreme Court.

Before we begin, I would like to acknowledge some people who have contributed to the success of this venture. Damon Linker of the University of Pennsylvania Press proposed this project to me at the beginning of the term and has supported it stalwartly since then. I thank him and the staff at the press for introducing me to the new world of e-books. My assistant, Shavaun O'Brien, can, I am convinced, do anything between a 10 a.m. emergency e-mail and lunch; she saved the project innumerable times. Dean Ron Weich of the University of Baltimore School of Law encouraged me to explore a new kind of legal scholarship. My University of Baltimore faculty colleague, Elizabeth Samuels, is as always a force for good in my work. My research assistants at the law school, Kristen Lim and Valerie Anias, provided crucial assistance, as did David Matchen and the rest of the staff of the University of Baltimore Law Library. In the final stage of writing, I took refuge in the Duke University Law Library; thanks to gracious hospitality from professors Paul Haagen and Dick Danner and Frances Conrad of the dean's office, it was idyllic. Kathy Bader was, as always, the perfect hostess during that frantic time.

As Supreme Court correspondent for the *The Atlantic Online*, I have worked with a number of talented editors, including Bob Cohn, John Gould, David Graham, Jennifer Rothenberg Gritz, Emma Green, Don Peck, and Scott Stossel. I was also lucky enough to gain admission to the court's press room and press gallery; the staff of the Supreme Court Public Information Office has been patient, generous, evenhanded, and good humored. In the press room, the brightest reporters in America decode the court's workings for the public. I am in awe of their care, thoroughness, fairness, knowledge of the law, and ability to make complex concepts clear. I must particularly thank Lyle Deniston of SCOTUSblog, who freely shared his matchless knowledge of court history and procedure. All these professionals have shown innumerable kindnesses to an academic interloper. I freely confess that I steal from them almost daily.

The Branch That Works

As late as Friday, there were rumors that the court might not open on time. Since 1917, the first Monday in October had been inviolate as the first day of the court's October term. But the Republican House and President Obama entered October seemingly locked in a death spiral. The Republican majority, impelled by its radical "Tea Party" wing, had returned from its summer recess with one demand: the president must agree to the repeal of his signature accomplishment, the Affordable Care Act (ACA). It was an extreme, almost surreal, demand. The Supreme Court had upheld the ACA—in most of its provisions—in June 2012. It had then been the major issue in the presidential and congressional elections of 2012, and the voters had, if not enthusiastically, decisively approved it. Polls showed that the voters—Republicans, Democrats, and independents— were dissatisfied with the act, but they wanted Congress to fix it, not repeal it.

But the Republican "base"—far to the right of the country or even Republican voters generally—wanted blood. A faction in the House blocked approval of new funding for the government and promised to restore it only when the Democrats agreed to total repeal of the ACA. It was as if Confederate generals had arrived at Appomattox Court House demanding Lincoln's resignation.

On October 1, 2013, the great shutdown began. Only essential federal workers were to report. The Capitol was nearly deserted. On October 3, the US Capitol police shot and killed a mentally disturbed woman who seemed to be trying to drive a car onto the grounds. Senators and house members cowered inside the building while the high-speed chase went on—protected by men and women whose paychecks they had blocked.

Just to the east of the Capitol, at the corner of E Capitol Street and First Street NE, the Supreme Court's marble palace loomed like a giant question mark. The court is an independent branch of government, of course, not subject to Congress's control. But as Alexander Hamilton had pointed out in 1788, it has neither "the sword nor the purse." Lyle Deniston, the dean of Supreme Court reporters, wrote in late September 2013, "Although the court does have awesome powers, it has no authority to print its own money." It would be a telling bit of symbolism if the court were not able to begin its October term on schedule—a visible sign that, in the words of scholars Thomas E. Mann and Norm Ornstein, "it's even worse than it looks."

In 2006, after his first term as chief justice, John Roberts discussed his ambitions for his tenure. "Politics are closely divided," he told journalist and scholar Jeffrey Rosen. "The same with the Congress. There ought to be some sense of some stability, if the government is not going to polarize completely. It's a high priority to keep any kind of partisan divide out of the judiciary as well."

Roberts took over the court in the fall of 2005. In his confirmation hearings, he assured senators that he believed in "judicial modesty." If he had his way, the court would serve as an umpire, not playing or deciding the game but simply calling "balls and strikes." But politics happened.

On January 20, 2009, Roberts administered the oath of office to Obama. With well over a hundred million people watching on television and the Internet, the two men muffed the Constitution's prescribed language. Afterward, commentators questioned whether Obama was actually president (the answer, specified in the Twenty-Fifth Amendment, was yes). The White House asked Roberts to make a hurried trip to 1600 Pennsylvania Avenue NW the next day to readminister the oath.

One year later, on January 21, 2010, the court upended American campaign finance law with its decision in *Citizens United v. Federal Election Commission* that, under the First Amendment, Congress could not forbid corporations from spending money to influence federal elections. A week after *Citizens United*, Obama came to the Capitol to deliver his annual State of the Union address. He had looked down at six members of the court seated before him in the well of the House of Representatives and said, "With all due deference to separation of powers, last week the Supreme Court reversed a century of law that I believe will open the floodgates for special interests—including foreign corporations—to spend without limit in our elections." Democrats reacted with thunderous applause.

Historians could not find another example of a president using the State of the Union to criticize the justices face to face. The episode had not pleased the chief. "To the extent the State of the Union has degenerated into a political pep rally, I'm not sure why we're there," he told an audience in Alabama a few weeks later. "The image of having the members of one branch of government standing up, literally surrounding the Supreme Court, cheering and hollering while the court—according the requirements of protocol—has to sit there expressionless, I think is very troubling." (A White House spokesman prolonged the nascent feud, telling reporters that *Citizens United*, not Obama's conduct, was "troubling.") The president has not confronted the court in his remarks again. As head of the judicial branch, Roberts has gamely continued to attend.

After *Citizens United*, partisan issues came thick and fast. The court continued its campaign against limits on money in politics. It loosened restrictions on state government aid to religious schools. It adjudicated a dispute over draconian state immigration laws, awarding partial victory to the federal government and partial victory to the states.

And in 2012, as the nation headed into a presidential election, the court confronted the ACA. The act contained an "individual mandate"—a requirement that each taxpayer provide health insurance for his or her household or pay a surcharge on income tax. When the act was passed, the mandate had been controversial, but largely as a matter of policy and politics, not of constitutional law. Afterward, a ferocious ideological blitz by conservative academics and well-funded libertarian groups had changed the discussion, making the mandate a symbol of "tyranny"—and convincing one federal Court of Appeals to void it. The issue reached the Supreme Court in March of 2012 and was decided on June 28, the last day of the court's term. The stakes could not have been higher. If the court struck down the mandate, the act might collapse. If it upheld it, the president could claim the justices' endorsement. Not only health policy but the outcome of the election might be at stake.

Whether by design or coincidence, however, the court had given the same verdict the country gave: it's a mess, it should be designed differently, but it's OK for now. Roberts had been the key—in a special opinion that gave neither wing of the court what it hoped for, he had upheld the "mandate" as a use of the taxing power.

Conservatives howled at what they saw as Roberts's desertion of their cause. There were, for the first time in memory, leaks from within the court about his "defection"—a sign that his colleagues on the right were deeply angered. One conservative talk-show host even suggested that Roberts' treason stemmed from the effects of medication he must take to prevent seizures.

Conservatives failed to notice that the constitutional doctrine that flowed from his separate opinion was far from liberal. The commerce power has been for a century Congress's main tool for regulating national matters. It reaches not only commercial regulation (food and drugs, for example, are "things" in interstate commerce, while trucks and airplanes are among its "instrumentalities") but environmental regulation (pollution's effects cross state lines and thus "affect" commerce "among the several states") and civil rights (race and sex discrimination in employment and public accommodation also "affect" commerce). But in *National Federation of Independent Business v. Sebelius*, the chief wrote that Congress could not use the commerce power to require that taxpayers insure themselves and their families. True, millions of uninsured Americans crowded the nation's emergency rooms. Under the law, they were entitled to emergency care, whether they could pay or not, and the resulting billions in expense profoundly distorted the health-care market. But nonetheless, the mandate was not a regulation of commerce but of "inactivity," and thus Congress was powerless to prescribe it. He did uphold the mandate as a tax—but the unprecedented "activity/inactivity" distinction was now the law, with potential results no one could anticipate.

The cutback in federal power did not stop there. Until *Sebelius*, it had been taken for granted that Congress could use the spending power to supplement its regulation of commerce. It could offer money to the states to carry out federal policy. The states could accept the money but needed to comply with federal mandates if they did. The ACA was designed to use this ordinary mechanism as a means of moving millions of low-income Americans out of the ranks of the uninsured. The bill raised the amount of money available to states to fund their Medicaid systems; if they accepted, the states were to expand eligibility to cover more of the "working poor." The federal government would pay 100 percent of the increased cost of the program for the first three years; then the amount would drop to 90 percent. It was a terrific deal for the states.

And that was the problem. Led by Florida, a number of Republican states made the strange argument that the offer was *too good*—that the federal government was becoming an organized-crime boss, "coercing" states by making an offer they couldn't refuse. Medicaid was a politically popular part of their state systems; they now had the choice of expanding the program or losing all their Medicaid funding. The latter was not likely—the secretary of Health and Human Services had discretion to work with states and provide waivers or partial reductions in cases where they didn't or couldn't. But at the urging of the anti-ACA faction, a majority of the court (including Justices Stephen Breyer and Elena Kagan) had suddenly created a new limit on the spending power. The federal government could no longer even threaten to cut off "existing" Medicaid funding—the money needed to run the old system it had abolished. That was a state entitlement, and if states chose not to expand the program, the government could do nothing.

Roberts' strange compromise moved the court out of the line of fire for the 2012 election. But the partisan issues kept coming. In the spring of 2013, the court gutted the Voting Rights Act of 1965, one of the chief achievements of the civil rights movement. Roberts wrote the opinion destroying the act's requirement that jurisdictions with a history of discrimination—mostly in the heart of the old Jim Crow South—gain approval from Washington before changing their election procedures. His opinion said, in essence, that racial discrimination was now a thing of the past. Since the act was passed in 1965, Roberts wrote, "voting tests were abolished, disparities in voter registration and turnout due to race were erased, and African-Americans attained political office in record numbers." Southern states were now oppressed by the "preclearance" section and deserved their freedom. The covered states responded with a flurry of laws making it harder for the poor, the elderly, and minorities to register and vote. Critics said that perhaps things had not changed quite as much as the chief had claimed.

The issue of same-sex marriage had roiled electoral politics for a decade. After the Massachusetts Supreme Judicial Court decided that same-sex couples had a right to legal marriage, state after state held referenda approving state constitutional bans on anything but the union of "one man and one woman." Before a single gay couple was allowed to wed, Congress weighed in by forbidding the federal government to recognize any same-sex unions. In June 2013, the court had (as with the ACA) split the difference. It struck down the federal Defense of Marriage Act (DOMA) and ordered the federal government to stop discriminating against same-sex couples legally married under state law, but it used a technical doctrine—"standing to sue"—to avoid ruling on Proposition 8, a California state constitutional amendment banning gay marriage. The DOMA opinion, however, convinced federal judges around the country that same-sex marriage was required, and state marriage bans started falling like dominoes around the country.

Would 2013 mark a break from the court's polarizing role? The first case on its docket was a fresh challenge to federal campaign regulations, one with the potential of changing the political playing field as sharply as *Citizens United.*

The attacks on the ACA continued, with a group of for-profit corporations demanding that they be allowed to withhold coverage of contraceptives from their employees despite the act's requirements. The corporations (the lead plaintiff was a family-owned chain called *Hobby Lobby*) claimed that providing the required coverage violated their right to the "free exercise" of their religion, which frowned upon some methods of contraception. Like the "inactivity" argument, the idea that corporations had "religion" and that commercial regulations could "burden" their "free exercise" was new. Again, whatever the court decided, a large part of the country and one of the political parties would be furious.

The court had agreed to hear a town government's plea for permission to impose Christian prayer on public meetings. Also on the docket was a fresh challenge to affirmative action and a case that took dead aim at public-employee labor unions.

At the outset of Obama's first term, the court had enjoyed the confidence of the public. In a Gallup poll before the October 2009 term, 61 percent of those surveyed approved of how it was doing its work, with only 30 percent disapproving. In late September 2013, however, only 46 percent approved, a statistically insignificant one point higher than the disapproval rate of 45 percent. Even the reasons for the trend were polarized: Thirty percent told Gallup that the court was "too liberal" while 23 percent said it was "too conservative." Roberts himself got good marks (55 percent in the fall of 2013), but the court was trending downward.

The government shutdown would last until October 17. But as SCOTUSblog's Deniston noted, the court must have found reserve funds in its budget somewhere. On the scheduled day, Monday, October 7, the nine justices emerged from behind the velvet curtain to hear the case of *McCutcheon v. Federal Election Commission*. While the rest of the government lay in suspended animation, the judicial branch was at work.

But if there was a swagger in the steps of the justices as they entered the courtroom, it may not have entirely been deserved. True, the court kept operating through thick and thin. (It was not unusual for the Supreme Court to hold oral arguments during blizzards that closed every other government office in Washington.) But was it entirely innocent during the creation of the partisan preening and thinly veiled hatred that poisoned the rest of the system?

In December 2000, the court had inserted itself into the 2000 presidential election and chosen the winner. In doing so, it put in office perhaps the single most polarizing political figure of our time, George W. Bush. Rich individuals and PACs, emboldened by the court's campaign finance decisions, have flooded the airwaves with ads that portray candidates and officeholders as evil, dishonest, dangerous, and almost satanic. No single force has done more to increase partisan hatred and suspicion than the toxic flood of anonymous electronic accusation and innuendo that now forms the core of American political campaigns. In 2004, the court was offered a chance to put limits on the computer-driven partisan reapportionment that is separating the House of Representatives into safe Republican and Democratic districts; it refused even to consider it. In 2008, the court also washed its hands of any limits on voter ID laws—more or less openly devised by Republican state legislatures to reduce turnout among Democratic voters.

In fact, as the court convened in October 2014, many state legislatures were at swords' point over an issue the court had created out of thin air: whether to expand Medicaid in line with the terms of the ACA. Had the court not created its new rule against Congressional "coercion," there would have been nothing to fight over.

No one who observes the chief justice would doubt that he was quite sincere in his wish for greater unanimity, greater judicial modesty, and a widely respected Supreme Court quietly calling "balls and strikes." But history shreds good intentions. Like any other political figure, the chief is limited by internal and external forces. The nation is divided; its legal system is also divided, no less than any other part. Lawyers across the country—some of them backed by almost unlimited funding from political and ideological groups—are working assiduously to destroy labor unions, health-care programs, environmental initiatives, and civil-rights protections. Other well-funded groups are determined to preserve precedents from earlier courts that furthered minority rights and increased protection for criminal suspects.

And the chief is only one of nine. Many of his conservative colleagues—particularly Justice Antonin Scalia, the senior conservative, and Justice Samuel Alito, the junior—are ready to reverse decades of precedent in pursuit of their conservative agenda.

Beyond that, it is a melancholy truth that human beings are capable of wishing for mutually incompatible things—order and freedom, for example, or safety and excitement. Both wishes may be sincere, but they may also be at war with each other. In his desire for harmony, acclaim, and hegemony, the chief was also fighting himself.

Ronald Reagan's spirit brooded day and night above the Roberts court. Its five conservative members all, in one way or another, owed their eminence to Reagan. Reagan appointed Justices Scalia and Kennedy. He plucked the young Clarence Thomas from obscurity and named him head of the Equal Employment Opportunity Commission, his first step toward to the high court. John Roberts and the young Sam Alito had been foot soldiers in the Reagan revolution, junior attorneys in the Reagan White House and Justice Department.

A decade after his death, the soft focus of historical memory has transformed Ronald Reagan into a cheering symbol of national esprit. But in life, he had been a polarizing figure. A rollback of civil-rights protections; an end to affirmative action; destruction of public-employee unions; deregulation of the economy and the environment; and sharp limits on (even abolition of) popular safety-net programs like unemployment compensation, Medicaid and Medicare, and even Social Security—these things were unpopular when Reagan championed them and no more popular in 2014 than they had been during the 1980s.

The question that loomed over the Supreme Court and its Reaganite majority was whether their hearts would lead them to write Reaganism into the law and the Constitution, finding for their leader a judicial victory in death to compensate for the complete political victory that eluded him in life. If the court took that path, then Roberts's "stability" might be postponed indefinitely.

Chapter 1

Balls and Strikes

Chief Justice John Roberts

McCutcheon v. Federal Election Commission

John Roberts, nominee for chief justice of the United States, appeared before the Senate Judiciary Committee from September 12 to 15, 2005. Roberts promised the senators, "I have no agenda, but I do have a commitment. If I am confirmed, I will confront every case with an open mind. I will fully and fairly analyze the legal arguments that are presented. I will be open to the considered views of my colleagues on the bench, and I will decide every case based on the record, according to the rule of law, without fear or favor, to the best of my ability, and I will remember that it's my job to call balls and strikes, and not to pitch or bat."

In his statement, he referred by name to two and only two figures from American history. The first was his predecessor, William H. Rehnquist, for whom he had served as law clerk during OT1980. Rehnquist had died a week earlier after battling cancer. "His dedication to duty over the past year was an inspiration to me and I know to many others," Roberts said. "I will miss him." The second was Ronald Reagan, who had brought Roberts to Washington a quarter-century earlier to serve as a junior attorney in the White House Counsel's office: "President Ronald Reagan used to speak of the Soviet Constitution," he said. "And he noted that it purported to grant wonderful rights of all sorts to people, but those rights were empty promises because that system did not have an independent judiciary to uphold the rule of law and enforce those rights."

Read closely, the references to Rehnquist and Reagan cut against the promise of humility. Neither the former chief justice nor the former president was especially modest in his aspirations for the federal judiciary.

Reagan's legal priorities, as set by his chief legal adviser, Edwin Meese, had included reversal of *Roe v. Wade*; a cutback on federal civil rights statutes (Reagan had opposed the establishment of a federal Martin Luther King holiday and unsuccessfully vetoed the Civil Rights Restoration Act of 1988) and in particular on the Voting Rights Act of 1965 (which he once called "humiliating to the South"); an end to affirmative action; and greater judicial tolerance for religion in government and public life. Reagan used the power of the presidency to crush a public-employee union, the Professional Air Traffic Controllers' Association, in 1981. Roberts, as a young Justice Department and later White House lawyer, was an enthusiastic part of the Reagan legal effort, writing memos critical of the Voting Rights Act and the Civil

Rights Restoration Act, skeptically viewing the protection of women under the equal protection clause, questioning constitutional protections for children of undocumented aliens, and championing an end to race-conscious affirmative action in federal hiring and contracts.

Reagan did get a chance to alter the court; he appointed three justices—Sandra Day O'Connor, Antonin Scalia, and Anthony Kennedy. He elevated Rehnquist, a Nixon appointee, to the chief's seat. Even before the ascension of Reagan, Rehnquist had campaigned actively against the prevailing doctrine of the Warren and Burger courts. As an associate justice, he was known as "the Lone Ranger" for his willingness to take solo positions that seemed far to the right of prevailing law. As chief justice, Rehnquist was not the Lone Ranger any more. But nobody ever called him an umpire.

In a 2006 interview, Roberts elaborated what he had learned from Rehnquist. "I think there's no doubt that [Rehnquist] changed, as associate justice and chief," Roberts said. "He became naturally more concerned about the function of the institution." As Lone Ranger, Rehnquist repeatedly criticized the police-warning requirements imposed by the Warren court case of *Miranda v. Arizona* ("You have the right to remain silent," etc.). But when, in 2000, the court had a chance to overturn the decision, Chief Justice Rehnquist not only voted to reaffirm it but wrote the opinion that did so. "He appreciated that it had become part of the law—that it would do more harm to uproot it," Roberts said, "and he wrote that opinion as chief for the good of the institution."

Roberts said his approach differed from Rehnquist's in one way, however: Rehnquist wanted to change the law and cared little about the margin. "I don't remember [promoting unanimity] as a feature that Rehnquist stressed much." Roberts said that he, by contrast, thought unanimity was good for the nation and the court. He hoped to foster "a culture and an ethos that says 'It's good when we're all together.'"

OT13 began with oral argument on a divisive, highly political case about campaign finance and concluded with two 5–4 decisions of divisive, highly political cases—one about public-employee unions and the other about contraceptive coverage under the ACA. In all three cases, the result furthered a high-profile objective of the Republican Party. In all three cases, the voting precisely followed the partisan makeup of the court, with the five Republican appointees voting one way and the four Democratic appointees bitterly dissenting. In all three cases, the chief voted with the hard-right position.

In between came a number of cases resolved by a vote of 9–0, thus no doubt gladdening the chief's heart. But underneath many of them was bitter disagreement about the reasoning of the unanimous result. The picture was so equivocal that the irrepressible Dahlia Lithwick, jurisprudence reporter for *Slate*, christened the new mood "fauxnanimity."

On the bench, Roberts is a somewhat contradictory figure. He is a far more genial presiding officer than Rehnquist, who (though unassuming in private) was a stern, even Saturnine presence on the bench. Largely stone-faced, Rehnquist allowed litigants no leeway when their time was completed. Roberts, by contrast, will frequently offer extra time for lawyers to complete their thoughts if the court has interrupted them often during oral argument.

Roberts is also sensitive of decorum in his court. When then Solicitor General Elena Kagan appeared in front of the court to argue *Robertson v. US ex rel Watson*, Justice Scalia asked her whether a federal prosecutor was an agent of the executive or judicial branch. "Who would you like the person be an agent of, Justice Scalia?" the cheeky Kagan responded. Roberts intervened—"Usually we have questions the other way"—prompting Kagan to apologize. In 2012, during the last of the interminable three-day, six-hour argument on the constitutionality of the ACA, Scalia began to riff on an old Jack Benny routine in which a robber says to Benny, "Your money or your life." The notoriously stingy comedian cannot decide. "You can't refuse your money or your life," Scalia said. "But your life or your wife's, I could refuse that one."

"No," the chief said, unsmiling. "Let's leave the wife out of it." When Scalia continued clowning, Roberts rebuked him sharply: "That's enough frivolity for a while."

As a writer, however, Roberts is both self-assured and good-natured. He delights in the written word; his prose is crystalline, vivid, and often humorous. In a 2008 opinion, he dissented from the court's denial of certiorari in a case about an arrest. He introduced the facts in the voice of a noir novelist: "North Philly, May 4, 2001. Officer Sean Devlin, Narcotics Strike Force, was working the morning shift. Undercover surveillance. The neighborhood? Tough as a three-dollar steak." In an OT09 case, AT&T argued that, as a corporation, it was a "legal person" and could thus refuse to disclose documents under a statutory provision protecting "personal property." Roberts wrote,

> In ordinary usage, a noun and its adjective form may have meanings as disparate as any two unrelated words. . . . [Thus] the noun "crab" refers variously to a

crustacean and a type of apple, while the related adjective "crabbed" can refer to handwriting that is "difficult to read"; "corny" can mean "using familiar and stereotyped formulas believed to appeal to the unsophisticated," which has little to do with "corn" ("the seeds of any of the cereal grasses used for food"); and while "crank" is "a part of an axis bent at right angles," "cranky" can mean "given to fretful fussiness."

The statute's "personal privacy" protection, he concluded, "does not extend to corporations. We trust that AT&T will not take it personally."

During OT13, Roberts authored four high-profile opinions in cases that concerned the federal government's power to make and enforce treaties, the states' power to protect abortion facilities from disruptive protest, the right of the police to search the contents of a cellphone when they have arrested its owner, and the federal government's power to limit contributions to federal election campaigns.

The campaign-finance opinion, called *McCutcheon v. Federal Election Commission*, was his signature work for OT13. The case followed the court's 2010 decision, *Citizens United*, in concluding that the First Amendment was an all but impassable obstacle to efforts to limit the role of concentrated wealth in politics.

Citizens United had dealt with the issue of "independent expenditures" by for-profit corporations during federal elections. The Bipartisan Campaign Reform Act ("McCain-Feingold") prohibited corporations from spending money to influence elections—in that case, by buying television time to advertise a film critical of then Senator

Hillary Rodham Clinton—within thirty days of the vote. The court concluded that Congress could put no limits on these "independent expenditures" by corporations, because they could not possibly create "corruption or the appearance of corruption." Everyone understood that they were *independent*. "Independent expenditures, including those made by corporations, do not give rise to corruption or the appearance of corruption," Justice Kennedy wrote for the majority. "The appearance of influence or access, furthermore, will not cause the electorate to lose faith in our democracy."

But *Citizens United* was simply one major battle in the conservative legal movement's long war against any limitations on money in politics. The court had specifically refused to discuss a different issue: whether *direct contributions*—where an individual or corporation puts a check into the outstretched hand of a political candidate— can be limited because of the interest in preventing corruption. Thus the stage was set for *McCutcheon*.

The specific issue in *McCutcheon* was whether Congress could enact "aggregate contribution limits" on political donors. Since the reforms of the 1970s, individuals may contribute to campaigns and party committees but only in limited amounts. (Direct contributions by corporations are forbidden, for now.) McCain-Feingold limited individual donors in how much they can give to individual candidates or party committees. These limits, called "base limits," were not at issue in *McCutcheon*. But the act also limited the "aggregate amount" any one donor could give to all federal candidates and committees in a given election cycle—a total of $48,600 to individual candidates and $74,600 to committees.

Shaun McCutcheon, an Alabama businessman, wanted to give more than that—he was maxed out on his aggregate limit but wanted to give contributions patriotically denominated $1,776 each to a total of a dozen more candidates during the 2014 cycle. He brought suit, alleging that the aggregate limits burdened his First Amendment rights.

Four justices of the court (Roberts plus Antonin Scalia, Anthony Kennedy, and Samuel Alito) agreed that the aggregate limits violated McCutcheon's rights; Clarence Thomas provided the fifth vote for McCutcheon but wrote separately to suggest that both base and aggregate limits are unconstitutional.

John Roberts wrote the opinion. It combines the best and worst of his judicial style. The prose is self-assured and clear. The legal conclusions are more debatable; the disregard for precedent is not. Roberts first brushed aside the court's first major campaign finance-reform case, *Buckley v. Valeo* (1976). That case held that "aggregate limits" were justified by the possibility that wily donors would use multiple contributions to "circumvent" the limits on direct contributions. That part of the *Buckley* opinion, he wrote, was only "a total of three sentences"—hardly worth noticing, really. He didn't overrule it; he made it disappear.

Without the *Buckley* precedent, Roberts then weighed the government interests at stake in the aggregate limits and found them, in essence, nonexistent. Congress, Roberts repeated, cannot seek to "'level the playing field,' or to 'level electoral opportunities,' or to 'equaliz[e] the financial resources of candidates.'" Thus, he said, its only legitimate reason for regulating campaign finance is "preventing corruption or the appearance of corruption."

Roberts, however, defined "corruption" only as what lawyers call "quid pro quo" ("this for that") corruption. That requires a bargain like, "I will give you $200,000 to vote for my subsidy." Roberts did not deny that the objects of McCutcheon's bounty were likely to feel grateful to him and to desire to please him while in office. This took the analysis back to *Citizens United*. In that case, the Court had noted that candidates who benefited from corporate "independent expenditures" might feel grateful to the corporations that made them. Once in office, they might even give those corporations special access. So what? "Ingratiation and access . . . are not corruption," Kennedy had written for the majority. Now Roberts applied the same logic to direct contributions. True, a candidate would feel grateful to McCutcheon and might be eager to please him, might give him special access, might consult him in preference to others who had not contributed. What's your point? asked Roberts in his opinion. That's not corruption; it's democracy at work.

"There is no right more basic in our democracy than the right to participate in electing our political leaders," Roberts began. "Citizens can exercise that right in a variety of ways: They can run for office themselves, vote, urge others to vote for a particular candidate, volunteer to work on a campaign, and contribute to a candidate's campaign. This case is about the last of those options."

McCutcheon, then, was seeking only his due as a citizen—the right to take part in politics. Aggregate limits discriminated against him by limiting the number of candidates he could support. Here is the heart of the opinion and perhaps of John Roberts's view of democracy:

> The individual may give up to $5,200 each to nine candidates, but the aggregate limits constitute an outright ban on further contributions to any other candidate. . . . At that point, the limits deny the individual all ability to exercise his expressive and associational rights by contributing to someone who will advocate for his policy preferences. A donor must limit the number of candidates he supports, and may have to choose which of several policy concerns he will advance. . . . It is no answer to say that the individual can simply contribute less money to more people. To require one person to contribute at lower levels than others because he wants to support more candidates or causes is to impose a special burden on broader participation in the democratic process.

As a matter of logic, this conclusion is demonstrably false. The limits do not require a donor "to contribute at lower levels than others"; they mean that, no matter how rich a donor may be, he or she can give no *more* than any other citizen. But Roberts meant something different: the donor limits meant that McCutcheon would be at a disadvantage among the other wealthy donors to a specific candidate. Some would be able to give the full amount, while McCutcheon would give less because he wanted to support more candidates.

This reasoning reflects a world in which giving money is the equivalent of voting and discrimination among those with money to give is the equivalent of—indeed, perhaps worse than—discriminating among voters. Consider the plight of Sean McCutcheon once he had given the maximum amount. He could volunteer for a candidate, Roberts wrote, but "personal volunteering is not a realistic alternative for those who wish to support a wide variety of candidates or causes." Beyond that, "other effective methods of supporting preferred candidates or causes without contributing money are reserved for a select few, such as entertainers capable of raising hundreds of thousands of dollars in a single evening."

The McCutcheons of the world, of course, are already members of a "select few." But that, to Roberts, was not enough. It was intolerable that *anyone* should have more influence than a wealthy donor: if Bruce Springsteen or Stevie Wonder could show support for a candidate by singing, then that discriminated against, subordinated, directly harmed rich people who could not. Having to give less than other donors to a specific politician was a very real harm to a wealthy person because the entire purpose of giving money was to gain friendship, access, and favoritism from the politician. And that, to Roberts, was as it should be; that was democracy at its best: "Government regulation may not target the general gratitude a candidate may feel toward those who support him or his allies, or the political access such support may afford. 'Ingratiation and access . . . are not corruption' [quoting *Citizens United*]. They embody a central feature of democracy— that constituents support candidates who share their beliefs and interests, and candidates who are elected can be expected to be responsive to those concerns."

Sean McCutcheon is simply a constituent, like the widow seeking help with her Social Security check. Of course, the widow has only her vote to offer as thanks. But Sean McCutcheon is rich; government cannot deny him the right to as much gratitude from as many politicians as he can buy.

In Roberts's view, the court was simply fulfilling its age-old role of protecting the lonely, endangered dissenter from an intolerant majority. "Money in politics may at times seem repugnant to some, but so too does much of what the First Amendment vigorously protects," he wrote. "If the First Amendment protects flag burning, funeral protests, and Nazi parades—despite the profound offense such spectacles cause—it surely protects political campaign speech despite popular opposition."

The Roberts view of democracy is the direct opposite of Justice Stephen Breyer's vision of "active liberty," in which the goal of the Constitution is to enable all citizens to participate in government. Breyer read a summary of his dissent from the bench on the day *McCutcheon* was decided: "Today's decision substitutes judges' understandings of how the political process works for the understanding of Congress, fails to recognize the difference between influence resting upon public opinion and influence bought by money alone, overturns key precedent, creates serious loopholes in the law, and undermines, perhaps devastates, what remains of campaign finance reform."

In his written dissent, Breyer laid out his view of the role of ordinary citizens in a democracy: "Campaign finance laws recognize that the First Amendment, which seeks to maintain a marketplace of political ideas and a 'chain of communication between the people,' and their representatives, cannot serve its purpose unless the public opinion it protects is able to influence government opinion. Campaign finance laws recognize that large money contributions can break that chain. When money calls the tune, those ideas, representing the voices of the people, will not be heard."

Roberts had dismissed the suggestion that committees could transfer funds to candidates, thereby getting around the "base limits" on contributions to individual campaigns. The chief justice suggested that the largely toothless Federal Election Commission could police these illicit transfers. Breyer responded dryly: "We react to [that claim] rather like Oscar Wilde reacted to Dickens's depiction of the death of Little Nell. 'One would have to have a heart of stone,' said Wilde, 'to read it without laughing.'"

Democrats found little to laugh about in *McCutcheon*, but Republicans and wealthy donors were exultant. The first major case of the term had been a total victory for the conservative agenda.

Chapter 2

Justice of Hearts

Justice Sonia Sotomayor

Dissenting, Schuette v. Coalition to Defend Affirmative Action by Any Means Necessary

On December 31, 2013, Sonia Sotomayor stood in Times Square and pressed a button to lower the famous ball, signifying to as many as one million revelers that the New Year had arrived. The entertainment card that night included rock stars Blondie and Melissa Etheridge, rapper Macklemore, and the scandalous twerking rocker Miley Cyrus. But Sotomayor was the headliner.

It's hard to imagine a bigger hometown honor for a girl from the Bronx than the Manhattan ball drop—but if there is one, Sotomayor has probably had it. Since 2010, this "Nuyorican" had been named to the Supreme Court, published a best-selling memoir, made a triumphant tour of the island where her parents was born, and appeared on

Sesame Street to adjudicate a dispute between Goldilocks and Baby Bear (the verdict from the bench: Goldilocks should fix the chair).

On New Year's Eve, Sotomayor also made headlines in her day job as a Supreme Court justice. She issued a temporary stay of a district court order requiring the Little Sisters of the Poor, an order of Catholic nuns, to provide government forms requesting exemption from the Affordable Care Act's contraception-coverage requirements. The Tenth Circuit had refused to stay the order; under Sotomayor's order, the nuns could refrain from filing until the issue was resolved before the Supreme Court. The back-to-back episodes showed two sides of this unusual justice: on the one hand, a deadly serious judge attempting to apply the law carefully; on the other, a full-fledged celebrity reaching out to a broader public.

She would turn sixty in the waning days of OT13. In that time period, she had risen from a childhood of poverty, disease, and dysfunction to the pinnacle of academic and professional achievement. Born in New York to Puerto Rican parents, she had been diagnosed with diabetes at the age of seven. Her father's hands shook when he tried to administer her insulin injections; he was an alcoholic and would die of drinking only two years later. Her mother had to be at her job as a practical nurse, so Sonia learned to inject herself.

After excelling in Catholic school, she graduated from Princeton and then Yale Law School. It was the dawn of the age of affirmative action, and Sonia was welcomed onto these elite campuses. She realized quickly that her background had not prepared her for life in the Ivy League. (Who, she wondered as an undergraduate, was this Jane Austen? And what was *Alice in Wonderland*?) She began a program of study on her own to give her the knowledge she did not have. Her determination paid off. She graduated summa cum laude and received the Pyne Prize, the university's top undergraduate academic award. At Yale she was an editor of the *Yale Law Journal*.

A recruiter from a top law firm made it clear that he considered affirmative action students unworthy; she complained to the university's career office, which forced the man to apologize. As an assistant Manhattan district attorney, she caught the eye of legendary DA Robert Morgenthau and Senator Daniel Patrick Moynihan. Moynihan told the George H. W. Bush White House that he would block their judicial nominations unless they gave one to his protégée; in 1991, Bush agreed to name her as a federal district judge. Seven years later, Bill Clinton named her to the Second Circuit. Republican senators fought the nomination bitterly because they recognized her potential to become the first Latina justice. She was confirmed in 1998, however, and in 2009, Barack Obama nominated her to the US Supreme Court.

Her way onto the court was not entirely smooth. Some advisers to the president urged him not to name Sotomayor, arguing that she lacked the academic brilliance of other potential nominees. "Bluntly put, she's not nearly as smart as she thinks she is," Harvard professor Laurence Tribe wrote to the president in 2009. (The letter was later leaked to the media, embarrassing both Tribe and Sotomayor.) After the resignation of David Souter, as Obama pondered whom to name, noted court commentator Jeffrey Rosen published an article entitled "The Case against Sotomayor," in which he quoted anonymous

New York lawyers and former Second Circuit clerks (for other judges). "The most consistent concern was that Sotomayor, although an able lawyer, was 'not that smart and kind of a bully on the bench,' as one former Second Circuit clerk for another judge put it," Rosen wrote. "'She has an inflated opinion of herself, and is domineering during oral arguments, but her questions aren't penetrating and don't get to the heart of the issue.'" Undeterred, Obama seized the chance to make history. On May 26, 2009, he nominated her in a White House event.

Republicans fought her confirmation in explicitly racial terms. During an academic event in 2001, Sotomayor had said, "I would hope that a wise Latina woman with the richness of her experiences would more often than not reach a better conclusion than a white male who hasn't lived that life." Before the hearings, Sotomayor said the comment was "a failed rhetorical flourish that fell flat." Republicans claimed it showed racial bias against whites. They also criticized her work with the Puerto Rican Legal Defense and Education Fund and a decision she had made on the Second Circuit upholding a city government's decision to discard the results of a promotion test that would have produced an all-white pool. (The case was criticized even by her Puerto Rican mentor, Second Circuit Judge Jose Cabranes, and later overturned by the Supreme Court.) But in the end, these qualms could not overcome the power of her life story, and the Senate confirmed the first Latina justice on August 6, 2009.

On the bench, Sotomayor soon eclipsed even Scalia as the court's most aggressive questioner. On some occasions, the chief justice or other justices would ask her to be quiet and allow a lawyer to respond. In her opinions, she was moderate to liberal, with some skepticism of local law enforcement; her opinions were somewhat long-winded and technical. She seemed on her way to establishing herself as a "judge's judge," a devotee of the inside language of jurisdiction and precedent. Off the bench, she embraced becoming a wider role model, particularly for young Latina women. Her memoir, *My Beloved World*, appeared in early 2013 and became a best seller. It is a vivid portrait of the impoverished but vital family and neighborhood that nourished her and of the struggles that took her to the bench. Its sales made her, for the first time in her life, moderately well-to-do. (She is by far the poorest justice.)

But there was one more distinction, which she earned five months later. Until April 22, 2014, Sotomayor had not read a dissent from the bench in the Supreme Court chamber. In her first four years on the bench, she had authored twenty-one dissents. In March 2014 she had even told former *New York Times* Supreme Court correspondent Linda Greenhouse that she didn't think much of dissents from the bench. "Announcing it from the bench," she said to Greenhouse in a public conversation at Yale Law School, "is like entertainment for the press."

Less than a month later, she reversed course in a case she clearly felt deeply about. No opinion she had written to date would gain more attention than the one she read in a case called *Schuette v. Coalition to Preserve and Defend Affirmative Action*.

Schuette arose out of the ongoing bitter battle against race-conscious affirmative action in college and university admissions. Many people believe that any use of race in the admissions process—even to open up institutions that were, until a generation or two ago, all white—disadvantages white people (and some other groups, like Asian Americans), stigmatizes nonwhites who "benefit" from it, and violates the equal protection clause of the Fourteenth Amendment.

The opponents of affirmative action lost a split decision at the Supreme Court in 2003. The court held, 5–4, that affirmative action in admissions was not unconstitutional, as long as race was not given a dispositive role in individual decisions. In 2006, one of the plaintiffs in that case, Jennifer Gratz, headed a coalition that put the issue to a popular vote. By a margin of 58 percent to 42 percent, Michigan voters enacted Proposal 2, an amendment to the state constitution. It forbade state schools to "grant preferential treatment to, any individual on the basis of race, sex, color, ethnicity, or national origin" in hiring, contracting, or education. Michigan's race-conscious admissions program was out of business.

Groups raced to the courthouse, arguing that an outright bar on affirmative action was a violation of equal protection clause. The lead plaintiffs were a coalition of civil rights groups called the Coalition to Defend Affirmative Action by Any Means Necessary, or "BAMN." The very name had a kind of anachronistic, sepia-tone quality: the phrase "by any means necessary" had been introduced into civil-rights discourse in 1964 by Malcolm X as an implicit rebuke to mainstream nonviolent civil rights leaders like Martin Luther King Jr. In a speech that year, Malcolm said, "We want freedom by any means necessary. We want justice by any means necessary. We want equality by any means necessary. . . . The time for you and me to allow ourselves to be brutalized nonviolently is passé."

The argument the group put forward seemed a bit like something out of the past as well.

The Sixth Circuit Court of Appeals, in a bitterly contested en banc decision, said that Proposal 2 violated something called the "political process doctrine" (or the "*Hunter-Seattle* doctrine"), which it summarized as saying that "minority groups may meaningfully participate in the process of creating [the] laws and the majority may not manipulate the channels of change so as to place unique burdens on issues of importance to them." The doctrine arose during the Warren and Burger courts in two cases that concerned popular votes abolishing programs to fight housing discrimination and promote school integration. Those earlier cases held that voters could not deliberately make it harder for minorities to make political or educational gains by amending state constitutions or local charters, repealing civil rights laws, and requiring new ones to gain majority approval.

The majority opinion seemed doomed from the start; the political process doctrine hadn't been invoked in nearly thirty years. In addition, affirmative action, by the court's own decree, could not be a program to help minority groups. It was there to assist the university in fulfilling its educational function.

There was a quasi-public struggle for control of the litigation between BAMN and a group of plaintiffs represented by prominent constitutional law scholars such as Laurence Tribe of Harvard. The two sides could not agree on who should argue before the Supreme Court. They ended up dividing their thirty minutes between BAMN's attorney and Mark Rosenbaum, an experienced advocate representing the other set of plaintiffs. That's usually a bad idea, because different lawyers may make self-contradictory arguments, leaving the justices with a muddled impression of the case.

The divisions among the plaintiffs were even more apparent when, on the weekend before oral argument, BAMN without notice dropped its designated attorney, an experienced Michigan appellate lawyer named George Washington, and substituted its own president, Shanta Driver. Driver had never appeared before the Supreme Court, but she came to the court seemingly determined to revive the rhetoric and jurisprudence of the 1960s. In her opening sentence, she asked the court "to bring the Fourteenth Amendment back to its original purpose and meaning, which is to protect minority rights against a white majority."

Justice Scalia at once interrupted. "So if you have a banding together of various minority groups who discriminate against—against whites, that's OK?" His comment shifted the moral onus onto BAMN—*they* were the ones who wanted to discriminate, this time against whites, he implied.

That charge is the heart of the conservative critique of affirmative action. Driver had attempted to ignore it. An experienced advocate would have seen that as dangerous. In fact, Driver never recovered the initiative. When the case was submitted, few people in the courtroom thought the Michigan program could survive. The only question seemed to be whether the court's conservative majority would use this unlikely vessel to outlaw affirmative action altogether. The court had been given that opportunity in OT12, in a case called *Fisher v. University of Texas*, and had taken a narrow path out of the thicket. Its majority held only that the lower court had not applied the proper test of race-based admissions programs. But affirmative action had, in form at least, survived, and Sotomayor had joined the six-justice majority opinion.

In late April, when the court announced its decision in *Schuette*, the lineup of votes was 6–2 (Justice Kagan had recused herself), but the coalition was quite different. Justice Breyer wrote separately that Proposal 2 was valid because the voters were not taking decisions about affirmative action away from elected officials but from administrators at universities. Justice Scalia, joined by Justice Thomas, wrote separately to repeat his long-standing belief that all affirmative action programs were unconstitutional, period. The key opinion was written by Justice Kennedy, joined by the chief justice and Justice Alito.

Kennedy began by announcing that the case was "not about the constitutionality, or the merits, of race-conscious admissions policies in higher education." He then announced what *was* at stake: the "right" of the majority to determine matters of racial policy. Of course the equal protection clause protected minorities, he said. However, "freedom does not stop with individual rights. Our constitutional system embraces, too, the right of citizens to debate so they can learn and decide and then, through the political process, act in concert to try to shape the course of their own times." Striking down Proposal 2 would be "an unprecedented restriction on the exercise of a fundamental right held not just by one person but by all in common."

It was a complete reversal of the claim Driver had unwisely made in October. For a generation, the court had insisted that equal protection rights were individual rights only, not the property of minority groups; now a new group right emerged—and it was a right of a majority to decide issues of race without interference from the courts.

On April 22, for the first time, the world heard Sonia Sotomayor's living voice in dissent. The dissent was powerful, angry, and pointed.

"For much of its history, our Nation has denied to many of its citizens the right to participate meaningfully and equally in its politics," she said. As a result, the court had evolved "a principle that is as elementary to our equal protection jurisprudence as it is essential: The majority may not suppress the majority's right to participate on equal terms in the political process." Proposal 2 did exactly that, she argued. Abdicating to the will of the majority marked a new turn in the court's jurisprudence—a new turn toward an old and ugly principle. "My colleagues are of the view that we should leave race out of the picture entirely and let the voters sort it out." That idea was "out of touch with reality, one not required by our Constitution, and one that has properly been rejected" in past cases.

In the personal core of the opinion, Sotomayor drew on her own experience and her own heart. The majority seemed to believe that America's race problem would be improved if courts simply ignored it. "Race matters," she wrote:

> Race matters for reasons that really are only skin deep, that cannot be discussed any other way, and that cannot be wished away. Race matters to a young man's view of society when he spends his teenage years watching others tense up as he passes, no matter the neighborhood where he grew up. Race matters to a young

woman's sense of self when she states her hometown, and then is pressed, "No, where are you really from?" regardless of how many generations her family has been in the country. Race matters to a young person addressed by a stranger in a foreign language, which he does not understand because only English was spoken at home. Race matters because of the slights, the snickers, the silent judgments that reinforce that most crippling of thoughts: "I do not belong here."

Sotomayor ended her dissent this way: "The way to stop discrimination on the basis of race is to speak openly and candidly on the subject of race, and to apply the Constitution with eyes open to the unfortunate effects of centuries of racial discrimination."

No one in the courtroom doubted that this cry of the heart was aimed at one member of the court—Chief Justice John Roberts, who had written repeatedly that affirmative action, not white racism, was the current problem in America's racial life. Advocates of civil rights were the ones creating racial tension, he had suggested. In an early voting-rights case challenging the racial makeup of majority-drawn legislative districts, he had written scornfully, "It is a sordid business, this divvying us up by race." Later he had written for a majority voiding a key portion of the Voting Rights Act on the grounds that Southern voting discrimination was in essence a thing of the past. And in a high-profile school desegregation case, he had blocked attempts by local school districts to ensure diversity in individual public schools. That opinion borrowed a phrase from an undelivered Ronald Reagan speech; it was now probably Roberts's most famous utterance: "The way to stop discrimination on the basis of race is to stop discriminating on the basis of race."

Sotomayor's dissent hijacked his words and read them back to him in a different form. Plainly stung, the chief hit back. Ordinarily, the function of a concurrence is to emphasize a point one justice believes the court's opinion has neglected or to seek to narrow the result beyond what other justices were willing to. But Roberts's concurrence in *Schuette* had one objective alone—to respond to Sotomayor in a tone of anguish and outrage:

> The dissent states that "[t]he way to stop discrimination on the basis of race is to speak openly and candidly on the subject of race." And it urges that "[r]ace matters because of the slights, the snickers, the silent judgments that reinforce that most crippling of thoughts: 'I do not belong here.'" But it is not "out of touch with reality" to conclude that racial preferences may themselves have the debilitating effect of reinforcing precisely that doubt, and—if so—that the preferences do more harm than good. To disagree with the dissent's views on the costs and benefits of racial preferences is not to "wish away, rather than confront" racial inequality. People can disagree in good faith on this issue, but it similarly does more harm than good to question the openness and candor of those on either side of the debate.

Roberts's color-blind rhetoric had resonated with a broad white public, weary of wrestling with America's historical guilt and defensive about implied accusations of racism. Now Sotomayor had put herself into this mix, insisting that the pain of racial division was not limited to white people but instead very much present in the lives of young blacks, Latinos, and others not part of white America.

Not long after her oral dissent, *New York Times* Supreme Court correspondent Adam Liptak published an analysis of the change in her role: "Sotomayor Finds Her Voice among Justices." Not only was she more confident on the bench but she had also become "a kind of folk hero to the adoring crowds who attend her public appearances by the thousands. . . . Some call her 'the people's justice.'"

Sonia Sotomayor seemed to have adopted a role that does not depend on majority vote, either in society or on the court. Like Antonin Scalia, she was learning to speak over the heads of her colleagues and over the heads of the law professors who had questioned her appointment. In her book, in her public speeches, and now from the bench, she would give voice to those who felt themselves excluded from the Roberts court's emerging jurisprudence of majority privilege.

She would become America's Justice of Hearts.

Chapter 3

Empathy for the Devil

Justice Antonin Scalia

Dissenting, Windsor v. United States (Redux)

On the night before the new term of court began, *New York Magazine* published an interview with Justice Antonin Scalia. Among the revelations in that discussion was this one: "I even believe in the devil."

The interviewer, reporter Jennifer Senior, asked Scalia to explain. But rather than answer her questions, Scalia used the expression he claimed to see on her face as an excuse for confrontation: "You're looking at me as though I'm weird," he said. "My God! Are you so out of touch with most of America, most of which believes in the devil?" Brushing aside her explanation, he went on, "You travel in circles that are so, *so* removed from mainstream America that you are appalled that anybody would believe in the devil!" She had, of course, said none of this.

The exchange captured Scalia's public persona, which he has carefully assembled during his nearly thirty years as a justice. Over and over, on the bench and the lecture circuit, he has insisted that his beliefs—religious, political, and legal—are those of "mainstream America" and that those who do not share them are out of touch with the ordinary people whose unelected tribune he claims to be. In an address to a Catholic group, he warned that "those who adhere to all or most of these traditional Christian beliefs are regarded in the educated circles that you and I travel in as, well, simple-minded." In an opinion on an antigay initiative in Colorado, Scalia wrote that "when the court takes sides in the culture wars, it tends to be with the knights rather than the villeins [commoners]."

And, as in the *New York Magazine* incident, he has been nothing short of brilliant in seizing the spotlight, establishing himself as a conservative hero. From the moment of his ascent to the court in 1986, he has managed to generate headlines with pungent phrases in his public appearances, telling one questioner to "get over it!" and responding to prochoice protesters with an indecent Sicilian hand gesture. He told one interviewer that the equal protection clause does not protect women from state-sponsored discrimination. During the run-up to the gay-marriage cases, Scalia was confronted politely by a gay student, who asked why the justice had seemed in earlier opinions to equate homosexuality with bestiality and murder. Scalia snapped, "If we cannot have moral feelings against homosexuality, can we have it against murder?"

Scalia's opinions—and in particular his dissents—have rarely failed to include one or two passages that are pungent, angry, and easily understood by ordinary

Americans. In a 2013 dissent in *Maryland v. King*, he protested the majority's approval of a state database of DNA results taken from suspects arrested on felony charges: "Perhaps the construction of such a genetic panopticon is wise. But I doubt that the proud men who wrote the charter of our liberties would have been so eager to open their mouths for royal inspection." In a 2011 case, *Brown v. Plata*, he objected to an order that California, having proven itself unable to give adequate medical care to its inmates, must release forty-six thousand of them. Of those released, he wrote, "many will undoubtedly be fine physical specimens who have developed intimidating muscles pumping iron in the prison gym." In a 1994 case, he wrote about injuries that capital defendants inflicted on their victims: "How enviable a quiet death by lethal injection compared with that!"

Scalia seemed to regard building the conservative movement—both in the law and in the nation—as part of his role as a justice. His success in that role stemmed from his own strong intellect and skill with words. Beyond that, it stemmed from his tireless campaign on behalf of the legal philosophy known as "originalism." This approach to constitutional interpretation was first devised in the 1980s with Reagan adviser Edwin Meese and conservative Judge Robert Bork. It holds that the sole role of a justice in constitutional cases is to ascertain the "original understanding" of a constitutional provision and apply it, regardless of changed circumstances.

Since his appointment in 1986 to the Supreme Court, this philosophy has had no more energetic or indefatigable spokesman than Scalia. "What I look for in the Constitution," Scalia wrote in 1997, "is precisely what I look for in a statute: the original meaning of the text, no matter what the original draftsmen intended."

"Often—indeed, I dare say usually—that is easy to discern and simple to apply," he continued. "Sometimes (though not very often) there will be disagreement regarding the original meaning; and sometimes there will be disagreement as to how that original meaning applies to new and unforeseen phenomena."

The quest for "original meaning" has led Scalia to champion some very conservative causes (expanded protection of gun rights, for example) and some that are less so (a strong interpretation of the Fourth Amendment's guarantee against "unreasonable seizures" and the Sixth Amendment's guarantee of a defendant's right "to be confronted with the witnesses against him"). It has given his jurisprudence a relentlessly backward-looking quality; history, to Scalia, answers most questions, and answers them, at least to his satisfaction, clearly.

In no area has Scalia's judicial pen been more pungent and memorable than in the court's ongoing encounter with the rights of gay men and lesbians. He came to the court just after *Bowers v. Hardwick*, in which a four-justice plurality upheld a state sodomy law on the grounds that disapproval of homosexuality has "ancient roots." He has left no doubt that he believed and believes that result to be correct, precisely because homosexuality *is* immoral and because Americans have historically thought it so. In 1996, by a vote of 6–3, the court struck down a Colorado initiative that proclaimed that gays and lesbians could never assert any legal "protected status or claim of discrimination." The law, Justice Kennedy wrote for the majority, had been passed "not to further a proper legislative end but to make [gays and lesbians] unequal to everyone else."

Scalia responded that "this court has no business imposing upon all Americans the resolution favored by the elite class from which the members of this institution are selected, pronouncing that 'animosity' toward homosexuality is evil." In 2003, the court, again by a vote of 6–3, overruled *Bowers* and proclaimed that states could not criminalize private, consensual sex between adult same-sex couples. Scalia again dissented, writing that the court majority "has largely signed on to the so-called homosexual agenda.... Many Americans do not want persons who openly engage in homosexual conduct as partners in their business, as scoutmasters for their children, as teachers in their children's schools, or as boarders in their home. They view this as protecting themselves and their families from a lifestyle that they believe to be immoral and destructive."

A decade later, during the October 2012 term, the court faced two cases implicating the possible right to same-sex marriage. In *Hollingsworth v. Perry,* a group of gay Californians asked the court to nullify Proposition 8, a state constitutional amendment, passed in 2008, forbidding same-sex marriage. Those plaintiffs, in effect, wanted the justices to proclaim a constitutional right to same-sex marriage. The court dodged that request, dismissing the case on jurisdictional grounds. But it decided the other case, *United States v. Windsor,* and Antonin Scalia's slashing pen was heard from in dissent.

Windsor was a challenge to a federal statute, the Defense of Marriage Act (DOMA), passed in 1996, that forbade the federal government to recognize any marriage between persons of the same sex, whether that marriage was recognized by a state or not.

Now a decade and a half later, eleven states and the District of Columbia were permitting same-sex couples to marry, and gay-rights advocates had found a dream plaintiff—a wealthy, elegant New Yorker named Edith Windsor whose longtime partner (and eventual wife) had died in 2009, leaving behind an estate so hefty that Windsor, the beneficiary of her will, had to pay state and federal governments more than $363,053 in estate taxes. If the federal government had recognized their marriage, Windsor's inheritance would have been free of tax.

The court's majority, again led by Kennedy, struck down DOMA. Marriage, it reasoned, had always been largely within "the authority and realm of the separate States." DOMA departed from that pattern, which was "strong evidence" that Congress sought to harm and stigmatize same-sex couples because of the majority's disapproval of their relationships. Under DOMA, legally married same-sex couples were deemed members of "second-class marriages for purposes of federal law." Even worse, the statute "humiliates tens of thousands of children now being raised by same-sex couples." The majority struck DOMA down, concluding that its "purpose and effect" were "to disparage and to injure those whom the State, by its marriage laws, sought to protect in personhood and dignity."

This opinion was the triumph for the "homosexual agenda" that Scalia had warned against a decade earlier in *Lawrence.* He penned a trademark dissent. The majority opinion, he wrote, meant the end of state laws restricting marriage to opposite-sex couples: "The real rationale of today's opinion, whatever disappearing trail of its legalistic argle-bargle one chooses to follow, is that DOMA is motivated by 'bare . . . desire to harm' couples in same-sex marriages. How easy it is, indeed how inevitable, to reach the same conclusion with regard to state laws denying same-sex couples marital status." As if unable to help himself, Scalia then took a passage of the majority's opinion and rewrote it to apply to a state same-sex marriage ban, outlining exactly how a future court would reason.

Many, if not most, serious dissents have one aim—to limit the damage done by the majority; point out the narrowness of the holding; hint broadly at ways that lower courts can read it narrowly; and suggest that another court, in the very near future, would think better of its mistake and restore the law to its previous state. The majority opinion could be read the way Scalia read it, but it was ambiguous and could have been read as affirming a state's right to approve same-sex marriage. If that was its actual its basis, then states could *deny* same-sex marriage as well. Chief Justice John Roberts, in a separate dissent, offered that interpretation of *Windsor*, suggesting that "the court does not have before it, and the logic of its opinion does not decide, the distinct question whether the States, in the exercise of their 'historic and essential authority to define the marital relation' may continue to utilize the traditional definition of marriage."

This was a valiant try, but Scalia and his vivid language grabbed the attention of the press, the public, and, as it turned out, lower court judges. During OT13, Scalia's angry words came home to roost. With stunning swiftness, federal district judges heard and decided challenges to state same-sex marriage bans. By May 2014, a dozen judges had struck down these bans—first in Utah, then in rapid succession, Ohio, Illinois, Virginia, Kentucky, and even Texas. Not one court upheld a state marriage ban. Judges young and old, male and female, gay and straight, Republican and Democrat, read *Windsor* and saw in it a logic that doomed the states' efforts to confine marriage to its "traditional" function as a union of man and woman. And some of what they cited was not in the majority opinion. In fact, about half of the opinions explicitly cited the Scalia dissent. A representative passage by Ohio District Judge Timothy Black stated, "And now it is just as Justice Scalia predicted—the lower courts are applying the Supreme Court's decision, as they must, and the question is presented whether a state can do what the federal government cannot—that is, discriminate against same-sex couples . . . simply because the majority of the voters don't like homosexuality (or at least didn't in 2004). Under the Constitution of the United States, the answer is no."

No words Scalia would write in the October 2013 term would have as much influence as the "prediction" he had written during OT12. That's because, disguised within the flamboyant rhetoric, he had made an important legal concession. Chief Justice Roberts had insisted that the majority was relying on federalism for its decision. If that was true, then judges might weigh the traditional state authority over marriage against the interests of same-sex couples and their children. But if Scalia's analysis was correct, if the majority had clearly held that opposition to same-sex marriage was based on a "bare desire to harm" gays and lesbians, a district judge would be required to adopt that analysis. It is hornbook equal protection law that a "bare desire to harm" cannot justify *any* law, whether aimed at gays and lesbians or any other groups. Scalia's dissent had strengthened the *Windsor* majority.

In the spring of 2013, Scalia was seventy-eight. Though his health appeared solid, he had visibly aged over his nearly three decades on the court. His face was now heavier, fleshy and florid. His behavior had begun to raise eyebrows: his manner on the bench had become more overbearing, while at the same time he seemed to be less prepared, less aware of the facts of the cases he was hearing. In a few cases his questions showed he simply did not understand the statutes he was construing. And his on-the-bench dissents had become even more extravagant than they had been before. In the spring of 2012, his oral dissent in an immigration case had suddenly turned into a bitter denunciation of the Obama administration's decision not to deport lawabiding alien children who had been brought to the United States as children—an issue that was not before the court. *New Yorker* correspondent Jeffrey Toobin wrote that that the harangue "marked his transition from conservative intellectual to right-wing crank."

Scalia's philosophy of "originalism" was showing its age too. Justice Alito, in particular, seemed to take pleasure in openly mocking it. Neither Alito nor Roberts cared much for precedent, and neither showed a burning curiosity about what the framers of the Constitution thought about anything. Alito and Roberts were young, and their jurisprudence looked ahead.

Scalia had always been the brains, the intellectual quarterback, of the conservative bloc. After OT13 that seemed no longer true. The three most important conservative wins were written by Roberts and Alito, and indeed Alito, by June, seemed to be the new ideologist for the Republican judges.

Scalia's most prominent appearance during OT13 was in a bitter *concurrence*, in which he agreed with the result of a case about the presidential "recess power" but excoriated Justice Breyer for not cutting that power back further. It was the first concurrence ever read from the bench as if it were a dissent. But that didn't make it any more significant.

When the final two blockbuster decisions were announced, they were conservative victories. Alito wrote and announced them, and Nino Scalia did not even appear on the bench. The empty chair underscored Alito's emergence—and Scalia's eclipse—as the brains of the court's right wing.

In his *New York* interview, Scalia mused on what future generations might think of his tenure. "For all I know," he said, "fifty years from now I may be the Justice Sutherland of the late-twentieth and early twenty-first century, who's regarded as: 'He was on the losing side of everything, an old fogey, the old view.' And I don't care."

In George Meredith's 1883 poem, "Lucifer in Starlight," the son of the morning, bored in hell, soars forth to cast a huge shadow over "Afric's sands" and "Arctic snows." But as he soars higher toward heaven, those domains recede, until at last,

> He reach'd a middle height, and at the stars,
> Which are the brain of heaven, he look'd, and sank.
> Around the ancient track march'd, rank on rank,
> The army of unalterable law.

Scalia has had nearly thirty years to alter the law, and in many ways, he has succeeded. Yet the pleasure of confronting error and forecasting doom has led him over and over into rhetorical excess. Scalia's *Windsor* dissent, written the year before, was probably his most influential opinion of OT13. It too was unalterable now, and it was doing its work in the lower courts. In fact, by June, it had begun to seem as if it might be remembered as the most influential opinion of his career—inadvertently cementing one of conservatism's most stinging defeats.

Chapter 4

Enter Laughing

Justice Elena Kagan

Dissenting, Town of Greece v. Galloway

During the first day of Elena Kagan's hearing before the Senate Judiciary Committee in 2011, South Carolina Senator Lindsey Graham tried to draw her out on the issue of national security. On December 25, 2010, "Christmas Bomber" Omar Farooq al-Nigeri had attempted to set off explosives in his underwear while aboard a Northwest Airlines flight from Amsterdam to Detroit. When Graham appeared to be alluding to the case, Kagan noted that she should not comment on "an undecided legal issue." Graham interrupted, "No, I just asked you where you were at on Christmas."

Without a discernible pause, Kagan responded, "Like all Jews, I was probably in a Chinese restaurant."

The hearing dissolved in laughter, and Graham's half-hearted attempt to box Kagan in was diffused. It was one of the more remarkable moments in Senate-hearing history; beyond that, it marked the emergence on a national stage of the newest Supreme Court justice—one blessed with a brilliant mind, razor-sharp wit, and the self-confidence to deploy both before the largest audience she would ever have.

The last Democratic nominee, Sonia Sotomayor, had been explicitly and repeatedly attacked on racial grounds by critics making a fuss about her use of the words "wise Latina." Using ethnic dog whistles against a Jewish nominee, however, is trickier. Senator Charles Grassley, the ranking Republican on the committee, attacked compliments Kagan had paid to Israeli Supreme Court Justice Aharon Barak, whose name came up repeatedly among Republican critics of her record because of his supposed "activism" on the Israeli bench. Kagan responded, "As you know—I don't think it's a secret—I am Jewish. The State of Israel has meant a lot to me and my family, and I admire Justice Barak for what he has done for the State of Israel in ensuring an independent judiciary."

Kagan had once written that modern judicial confirmations are marked by "vacuity and farce." Her performance was not vacuous or farcical, but it was funny. Nobody laid a glove on Elena Kagan.

Even though her nomination was opposed by gun-rights and anti–gay marriage groups, she was confirmed 63–37. Immediately after the vote, Robert Barnes of the *Washington Post* later reported, John Roberts phoned to welcome her to the court. They would, he said, be serving together over the next twenty-five years.

"Only twenty-five?" she asked.

Enter Kagan, laughing.

She arrived on the court with an unusual resume. She was the first nominee in four decades who had not previously served as a judge. She had, in fact, barely practiced law at all; until Obama appointed her solicitor general in 2009, she had argued only a few preliminary motions before trial courts. It was, however, a brilliant career. Manhattan upbringing, the daughter of a tenants' rights lawyer and a schoolteacher (both her brothers became public-school teachers as well). Summa cum laude from Princeton, master's degree at Oxford, JD magna cum laude from Harvard Law School. Clerkships with two liberal icons—Abner Mikva of the DC Circuit and Justice Thurgood Marshall of the Supreme Court. (Marshall, who liked to nickname his clerks, dubbed the diminutive Kagan "Shorty.") Tenure at the University of Chicago within four years, then policy and legal positions in the Clinton White House.

In 2003, at the age of forty-three, she was named dean of Harvard Law School. Harvard at the time was in a slump, all but paralyzed by factional fighting and scholarly doldrums. By the time she left in 2009, Harvard had revamped its first-year curriculum and hired more than forty new faculty members. The school had entered a new era of peace, and grizzled Harvard scholars were eating out of her hand.

In fact, wherever she went, Elena Kagan inspired legions of admirers. Her winning ways continued on the court. She attended operas and aerobics workouts with Ruth Bader Ginsburg, she learned to hunt under the tutelage of Nino Scalia, and she made joint appearances with Clarence Thomas.

Justices often struggle during their first few terms to fashion a judicial role and voice. From her very first opinion, in an undistinguished bankruptcy case called *Ransom v. FIA Card Services*, Kagan, like Roberts, displayed an ability to take a complex issue ("whether a debtor . . . who owns his car outright, and so does not make loan or lease payments, may claim an allowance for car-ownership costs [thereby reducing the amount he will repay creditors]") and render it in English so clear that even a nonlawyer, if so minded, could understand. Her first dissent, during OT10, likewise showed not a hint of diffidence.

That case was called *Arizona Christian School Tuition Organization v. Winn.* At issue was a scheme devised by the Arizona legislature to funnel state funds to private schools. Taxpayers could donate to "tuition organizations" that funded scholarships at private schools. The taxpayers could then take a tax credit—reducing their taxes dollar for dollar—for the donation. The "tuition organizations," meanwhile, could decide to fund scholarships only at specific schools, including schools of a certain religious denomination. Thus a taxpayer would know that the scholarships would benefit only students at Christian schools.

The court majority, in an opinion by Kennedy, held that there was no violation of the establishment clause. The donations came from individuals, and the tax credits the donor later got did not turn the donations into state funds, Kennedy reasoned. Kagan dissented: "Suppose a State desires to reward Jews—by, say, $500 per year—for their religious devotion. Should the nature of taxpayers' concern vary if the State allows Jews to claim the aid on their tax returns, in lieu of receiving an annual stipend? . . . The court today [approves that scheme], but that is wrong." The dissent was pointed but good humored. That describes Kagan on the bench as well. She is usually smiling and seems absorbed in the details of the case before her. As a judicial questioner, she tends to focus on the big picture presented by a case. A characteristic Kagan question begins, "Aren't you really saying . . . ?"

Here, for example, is a question she asked during oral argument in an OT13 case called *Town of Greece v. Galloway.* Legal scholar Douglas Laycock, representing a group of religious dissenters, was asking the court to order an end to specifically Christian prayers at the beginning of town council meetings in the small upstate New York town of Greece. "Mr. Laycock," Kagan asked, "all hypotheticals aside, isn't the question mostly here in most communities whether the kind of language that I began with, which refers repeatedly to Jesus Christ, which is language that is accepted and admired and incredibly important to the majority members of a community, but is not accepted by a minority, whether that language will be allowed in a public town session like this one. That's really the question, isn't it?"

Laycock agreed. Kagan continued, "I don't think that this is an easy question. I think it's hard, because of this. I think it's hard because the court lays down these rules and everybody thinks that the court is being hostile to religion and people get unhappy and angry and agitated in various kinds of ways. . . . Part of what we are trying to do here is to maintain a multireligious society in a peaceful and harmonious way. And every time the court gets involved in things like this, it seems to make the problem worse rather than better. What do you think?"

Laycock politely disagreed that the court would inevitably make things worse. But when the court decided his case six months later, it made a remarkable change in the law—one that he most probably did not welcome.

Until 1999, the Greece Town Council had opened its monthly meetings with a moment of silence. But John T. Auberger, a newly elected town supervisor, wanted prayer. At first Auberger led the prayers himself; then the council began inviting local clergy to give prayers. Over a thirteen-year period, all but three of the clergy invited were Christian ministers. Many asked the audience to bow their heads, called on Jesus Christ, led a group recital of the Lord's Prayer, or asked the audience to say "Amen."

The court had previously upheld "legislative prayer" before meetings of bodies like the Senate or a state legislature. That means prayer directed at the body's own members to solemnize the opening of a business day. That kind of prayer was approved by a 1983 case, *Marsh v. Chambers*. The court in *Marsh* relied on history to reject a challenge to prayers in front of Nebraska's legislature, "where . . . there is no indication that the prayer opportunity has been exploited to proselytize or advance any one, or to disparage any other faith or belief."

But there are crucial differences between the Nebraska chaplain's invocations and those at the town-board meetings in Greece. To begin with, onlookers in Nebraska were in a gallery while the chaplain addressed the members of the legislature. No citizen was called on to do business with the legislature during its session. And the chaplain, after first referring to Jesus in his early prayers, stopped the practice when a Jewish member quietly objected.

In Greece, moreover, citizens come to the town board not only to watch but to apply for building permits and zoning changes. The "chaplain of the month" faces the audience, not the members, and often aggressively asks attendees to bow their heads and pray. As Kagan had noted in her question, the prayers are rife with theological claims not only controversial to non-Christians but troubling for many of the faithful. (Those three non-Christian "chaplains" were picked just after litigation over the prayers began, and the nod has gone to Christians for the six years since.)

Faced with the *Marsh* precedent, the challengers did not ask the court to ban the opening prayers altogether. Instead, they asked that "prayers that are obviously sectarian . . . should be prohibited."

They were picking up on a suggestion offered twenty years ago by Justice Scalia in a dissent over prayer at a high-school graduation. The majority held such prayers forbidden because they indirectly coerced the students and their families to engage in religious observance. Scalia ridiculed that idea. He argued that the establishment clause actually rules "out of order government-sponsored endorsement of religion . . . where the endorsement is sectarian, in the sense of specifying details upon which men and women who believe in a benevolent, omnipotent creator and ruler of the world are known to differ (for example, the divinity of Christ)."

But the "nonsectarian" argument was a nonstarter in front of the contemporary court. In May 2014, the majority rejected the very idea of "nonsectarianism." The legislature could not monitor prayer for its sectarian content,

Kennedy wrote. "Government may not mandate a civic religion that stifles any but the most generic reference to the sacred any more than it may prescribe a religious orthodoxy." Despite what Scalia had written two decades ago, Kennedy wrote, "There is doubt . . . that consensus might be reached as to what qualifies as generic or non-sectarian." Kennedy's opinion admitted that some prayers will discomfit some dissenting citizens. "Offense, however," he wrote, "does not equate to coercion."

But even with the new green light, local legislative prayer will not become a free-for-all call to Jesus, Kennedy continued: "If the course and practice over time shows that the invocations denigrate nonbelievers or religious minorities, threaten damnation, or preach conversion . . . that circumstance would present a different case than the one presently before the court."

In other words, legislators need not—indeed constitutionally cannot—monitor prayers for sectarian content. The courts, however, can monitor all the prayers as a group if someone brings a lawsuit.

Kagan's dissent was her highest-visibility opinion to date. It was joined by Ginsburg, Breyer, and Sotomayor. Her opinion was built around one idea: "When citizens go before the government, they go not as Christians or Muslims or Jews (or what have you), but just as Americans." The promise of inclusion, she wrote, is betrayed when government requests individuals to join in the prayer of one religion. A dissenter at that moment becomes "a different kind of citizen," who "stands at a remove, based solely on religion, from her fellow citizens and her elected representatives."

At the outset, she gently accused the majority of bad faith. Kennedy's decision pretended that the Greece prayer scheme had been open to all faiths and citizens. The record showed the contrary—except for three occasions immediately after the lawsuit began, every invited chaplain had been Christian. The town also had not advertised any way for clergy or citizens to volunteer. The Christian invokers in Greece were determinedly, almost pugnaciously, "sectarian." In fact, when the plaintiffs first complained, the council stood by while an invited invoker told God that "they are in the minority, and they are ignorant of the history of our country." The majority opinion simply pretended that these flaws were not really there.

The town was picking its prayers, and they were prayers to the God favored by Auberger and his fellow board members, Kagan wrote:

> Suppose . . . that government officials in a predominantly Jewish community asked a rabbi to begin all public functions with a chanting of the Sh'ma and V'ahavta. ("Hear O Israel! The Lord our God, the Lord is One. . . . Bind [these words] as a sign upon your hand; let them be a symbol before your eyes; inscribe them on the doorposts of your house, and on your gates.") Or assume officials in a mostly Muslim town requested a muezzin to commence such functions, over and over again, with a recitation of the Adhan. ("God is greatest, God is greatest. I bear witness that there is no deity but God. I bear witness that Muhammad is the Messenger of God.")

If, reading those words, her colleagues felt left out of the religious dialogue (the words "Sh'ma," "V'ahavta," or "Adhan" had never before appeared in a Supreme Court opinion; one wonders how many of the justices had actually encountered them in any context), that was, her tone implied, exactly how outsiders at the town board meetings felt when the "chaplain of the month" asked them to stand and address words of faith to the savior, Jesus Christ.

"Let's say that a Muslim citizen of Greece goes before the board to share her views on policy or request some permit," she wrote. When the designated chaplain asks citizens to pray to Jesus, "she faces a choice—to pray alongside the majority as one of that group or somehow to register her deeply felt difference." If she were to refuse to stand or even to leave the room (as the majority had suggested), "she becomes a different kind of citizen, one who will not join in the religious practice that the town board has chosen as reflecting its own and the community's most cherished beliefs. And she thus stands at a remove, based solely on religion, from her fellow citizens and her elected representatives. Everything about that situation, I think, infringes the First Amendment."

Kagan did not argue that the town board should not open with prayer; instead, she called for "the recognition that we are a pluralistic people too" and that "government must take especial care to ensure that the prayers [at meetings] will seek to include, rather than serve to divide." Clergy could be asked to pray in an inclusive way or at least to tell onlookers they were free not to take part in prayer, she suggested. Or the board could actually invite representatives of different faiths in a dependable rotation, instead of just pretending to. "When one month a clergy member refers to Jesus, and the next to Allah or Jehovah," she wrote, "the government does not identify itself with one religion or align itself with that faith's citizens, and the effect of even sectarian prayer is transformed." The majority had dismissed the objections of religious dissenters as mere "offense," a kind of personal quirk. "Adults often encounter speech they find disagreeable," Kennedy wrote, "and an establishment clause violation is not made out any time a person experiences a sense of affront from the expression of contrary religious views."

Kagan attacked that reasoning head on: "The not-so-implicit message of the majority's opinion—'What's the big deal, anyway?'—is mistaken. The content of Greece's prayers is a big deal, to Christians and non-Christians alike. A person's response to the doctrine, language, and imagery contained in those invocations reveals a core aspect of identity—who that person is and how she faces the world.... I would treat more seriously the multiplicity of Americans' religious commitments, along with the challenge they can pose to the project—the distinctively American project—of creating one from the many, and governing all as united."

She might lack the votes now; she might never have the votes. But Kagan's career to this point promised that she would bear witness to these values—directly and firmly—in the voice of an outsider who understood, in a way some of her colleagues seemed unwilling or unable to do, the real stakes in disputes about government's relationship to God.

How long would that be? More than twenty-five years, she had promised Roberts. Kagan's *Greece* opinion appeared the week after her fifty-fourth birthday. In twenty-five years, she would be about the age that Scalia and Kennedy were at the end of OT13. She might have the last laugh.

Chapter 5

Big Brother

Justice Anthony Kennedy

Hall v. Florida

An old joke asks how many Harvard Business School graduates it takes to change a light bulb. The answer is "One. He holds up the bulb and the universe revolves around him."

That quip might be a metaphor for Anthony Kennedy's role on the Roberts court. Lewis F. Powell Jr. and Sandra Day O'Connor were "swing votes"; they agonized over legal principle and factual nuance before deciding on an approach to a case. Kennedy does not agonize.

In some areas, such as federal-state relations or affirmative action, he is highly conservative. In others, particularly matters involving gay rights and the rights of young people, he seems liberal. What he very rarely appears to be is in doubt. His single vote often affects which way the court goes. But that is not the same thing as wavering. The court revolves around him.

Despite his apparent divergences from the conservative line, Kennedy is in no way a moderate. He is a man of conservative views and deep religious feeling. But he is not a "movement conservative"; he is quite independent.

Kennedy turned seventy-eight in July 2014, just after the close of the term. He is perhaps the last justice who would ever come to the court from the vanished age when a lawyer was an independent, learned professional who offered a detached, broad view of the problems of the community.

Born in 1936, Kennedy grew up in Sacramento, California. Though Sacramento is the capital of the nation's most populous state, it is still a city of fewer than half a million souls. When Kennedy was born, its population numbered roughly one hundred thousand—fewer, at the time, than small towns like Richmond, Virginia, or Grand Rapids, Michigan. His father, Anthony Kennedy Sr., was a lawyer with a solo practice focusing largely on work for private clients, including lobbying the California State Legislature. Politics ran in the family; ten-year-old Anthony Jr. took a year off from school to serve as a page in the state Senate.

Kennedy's academic career was superlative—public high school, Stanford undergraduate, a Harvard Law degree; he began law practice in 1961 with an associate's spot at a San Francisco firm. But two years later, the elder Kennedy died, and young Tony Kennedy returned to the town and the house of his birth, where he would remain until he left in 1987 for the US Supreme Court. He took over his father's practice, a kind of practice that barely exists anymore in major cities and that is unlikely ever to produce a Supreme Court justice again.

"Lawyers know life practically," Samuel Johnson once said. "A bookish man should always have them to converse with." Kennedy, like so many small-town lawyers, was both practical and bookish. His practice exposed him to his clients' human and financial problems; in the evenings, he was (and remains) a voracious reader of fiction and nonfiction alike.

Unlike his five Republican colleagues on the court, Kennedy never accepted any appointive political office or, before taking the bench, received a government paycheck. He never worked on the staff of any politician. He did not join organizations like the Federalist Society. As a lawyer or lobbyist, he was involved in Republican politics but as an independent figure offering service and advice. As a friend of then Governor Ronald Reagan and his legal adviser, Edwin Meese, he helped craft a statewide tax limitation measure that Reagan placed on the ballot in 1973. It failed. In 1975, President Gerald Ford appointed him to the Ninth Circuit. He moved his office to the federal courthouse and continued to live in the house he was born in.

In 1987, Reagan reentered his life with a nomination to the Supreme Court. It would, of course, be impossible for any lawyer not to be grateful for the honor. But the gratitude must have been mutual. When the White House came to Kennedy that year, Reagan was in political trouble. His first nominee, Robert Bork, had been rejected by the Senate. The second choice, Judge Douglas Ginsburg of the DC Circuit, had withdrawn his name after news reports revealed he had been a user of marijuana during his years as a professor at Harvard Law. The administration needed a nominee who could glide to confirmation, and they needed that nominee fast. Kennedy thus arrived on the bench as he had lived, owing little to anyone. It's not odd that he brought with him a largely independent, highly conservative sense of the law and a justice's role.

Unlike Scalia or, in later years, Alito, Kennedy's questions are relatively few and virtually never tinged with hostility or rudeness. He usually asks each advocate one or two questions designed to probe the heart of the case as he sees it and sometimes helpfully asks, "What is the best case for your side?" During many oral arguments, he will ask what some called the Kennedy Question—one that reveals which way the justice is leaning. In the landmark gun-rights case *District of Columbia v. Heller*, for example, he asked the lawyer defending DC's handgun ban whether the Second Amendment's "right to bear arms" arose out of "the concern of the remote settler to defend himself and his family against hostile Indian tribes and outlaws, wolves and bears and grizzlies and things like that?"

The historians' answer to that question would have been "no," but almost everyone in the chamber assumed that Kennedy's was "yes." And as a Westerner, he would be opposed to any limits on the rights of Western settlers. That impression was confirmed three months later when Kennedy contributed the crucial fifth vote to an opinion finding, for the first time, an individual "right to bear arms."

Central to Kennedy's judicial thought is a concept of "dignity," of the inviolable private liberty of the individual, and of a sense that the state should not insert itself into certain intimate areas of life—particularly the lives of gay men and lesbians, as well as the marriages they enter into and the families they create. He has three times ridden to their judicial rescue.

In the 1996 case of *Romer v. Evans*, he wrote for a six-justice majority that the voters of Colorado could not amend their state constitution to bar "homosexual, lesbian or bisexual orientation, conduct, practices or relationships" from attaining "minority status, quota preferences, protected status or claim of discrimination." The final word was the important one: the Colorado amendment voided all state and local antidiscrimination laws that covered gays and lesbians. The amendment, Kennedy wrote, "seems inexplicable by anything but animus toward the class that it affects." It was invalid because a "state cannot so deem a class of persons a stranger to its laws."

In *Lawrence v. Texas*, he again embraced the "autonomy of self that includes freedom of thought, belief, expression, and certain intimate conduct." His opinion, supported by five votes, voided a Texas law that outlawed "deviate sexual intercourse with another individual of the same sex." (Justice O'Connor concurred, bringing the vote total to six, but on a different ground.) Kennedy drew together comparative law, international human rights law, and cutting-edge work in gay history to conclude that the court should overrule its 1986 decision in *Bowers v. Hardwick* that a state could outlaw gay sex because of moral disapproval by the majority. "Its continuance as precedent demeans the lives of homosexual persons," he wrote. "The petitioners are entitled to respect for their private lives. The State cannot demean their existence or control their destiny by making their private sexual conduct a crime."

Most recently, in June, 2013, Kennedy had electrified the nation by writing (for himself and Ginsburg,

Breyer, Sotomayor, and Kagan) that section 3 of the federal Defense of Marriage Act (DOMA) was an unconstitutional violation of Fifth Amendment equal protection. That law barred the federal government from recognizing state-sanctioned same-sex marriages. "The act's demonstrated purpose is to ensure that if any state decides to recognize same-sex marriages, those unions will be treated as second-class marriages for purposes of federal law," he wrote. That distinction "demeans the couple" and "humiliates tens of thousands of children now being raised by same-sex couples."

The reference to children illustrated a key part of Kennedy's jurisprudence. Kennedy likes to throw a protective arm over the shoulders of the innocent and unprotected—those who might need a big brother to help them. Whatever anyone might think of same-sex couples, no one could accuse their children of immorality or anything else.

Children in general were a special focus of his benevolence. In *Roper v. Simmons*, he wrote for five justices that states could not put defendants to death for crimes they had committed as juveniles. In 2010, he wrote another 5–4 opinion holding that juvenile offenders could not be sentenced to life without parole for anything but homicide; in 2012, he voted with the liberals (Kagan wrote the opinion) to hold that states could not use life without parole against juveniles even in murder cases.

Kennedy's vote had robbed the conservative movement of the victory it most wanted—an end to *Roe v. Wade*. In the 1992 case of *Planned Parenthood of S.E. Pennsylvania v. Casey*, he sided with Justices Sandra Day O'Connor and David H. Souter in an opinion that limited abortion rights without wiping them out. That opinion seemed to be based on a respect for the court's role and the doctrine of precedent rather than his views on abortion or women's autonomy. Despite his vote in *Casey*, Kennedy seemed to feel that adult women were more in need of protection than of liberty. In the 2007 case of *Carhart v. Gonzales*, he upheld a ban on so-called partial-birth abortions as a way of protecting women from later regretting their own mistakes. "While we find no reliable data to measure the phenomenon, it seems unexceptionable to conclude some women come to regret their choice to abort the infant life they once created and sustained," he wrote. "Severe depression and loss of esteem can follow." A partial-birth abortion ban would at least spare them the later sorrow of knowing they had chosen a form of abortion that some considered brutal.

Not only children and women but the intellectually disabled seemed to call out his gallantry. In the 2002 case of *Atkins v. Virginia*, Kennedy voted with the majority that, under the Eighth Amendment, states could not put "mentally retarded" killers to death. In OT13, Kennedy again got a chance to play the protective brother to these defendants (now legally called "intellectually disabled").

Hall v. Florida was a test of the court's holding in *Atkins*. After *Atkins*, the Florida Supreme Court had purported to apply the decision by creating a hard-and-fast rule: any defendant who tested above seventy on an IQ test was *not* "retarded," the state court held, and thus could not even offer any clinical evidence of intellectual disability.

That rule—followed by eight states—defies the clinical definition of "intellectual disability" (the preferred term). The average IQ score, by definition, is one hundred.

Psychologists define a seriously subnormal score as greater than two "standard deviations" below the average—in other words, seventy or lower. But simply scoring seventy on a test doesn't mean that a patient's "true" IQ is seventy. An IQ score by itself, professionals agree, can't be conclusive one way or the other. Designers of IQ tests know their test scores are subject to a "standard error of measurement," or SEM, which reflects how closely the text reflects the test taker's hypothetical "true score." For standard IQ tests, the SEM is about five points one way or another. That means that a single score of seventy makes it 95 percent likely the "true score" is between sixty-five and seventy-five.

A mental-health professional combines IQ data with two other pieces of information: (1) how much trouble the patient has experienced in adapting to the stresses of daily life and (2) when the patient's troubles began. (Intellectual disability is a "childhood-onset" condition, manifesting itself soon after birth.) A combination of the three bits of data can produce a diagnosis of disability.

In *Atkins*, the court told death-penalty states to develop procedures for diagnosing disabled defendants. The Florida Supreme Court responded by reading state law as requiring a score below seventy; even one point higher and a defendant was barred from producing clinical evidence of the other two factors. It was not a rule any mental-health professional would approve.

By an accident of evidence law, Freddie Lee Hall found himself on the wrong side of the Florida line. In the years since his conviction for murder, he had in fact scored as low as sixty on IQ tests; the state court, however, held that the lower scores were not admissible in evidence. The lowest score that made it into the record was seventy-one.

The crime Hall and another man committed was brutal. They kidnapped, beat, and raped a twenty-one-year-old pregnant woman; later the same day, they shot and killed a Florida sheriff's deputy. But the facts of his life (ruled inadmissible by the state court) were also agonizing. Kennedy's opinion summarized those facts: Hall was "constantly beaten because he was 'slow' or because he made simple mistakes." His mother "would strap [Hall] to his bed at night, with a rope thrown over a rafter. In the morning, she would awaken Hall by hoisting him up and whipping him with a belt, rope, or cord." Hall was beaten "ten or fifteen times a week sometimes." His mother tied him "in a 'croaker' sack, swung it over a fire, and beat him," "buried him in the sand up to his neck to 'strengthen his legs,'" and "held a gun on Hall . . . while she poked [him] with sticks."

At oral argument, Florida's lawyer argued that the Constitution did not require the state to consider this evidence if it was satisfied with the IQ test. The Eighth Amendment doesn't require a state to "adopt all kinds of—of clinical criteria," he said. A rule was a rule; if the state courts said he wasn't disabled, he wasn't.

The Kennedy Question in *Hall*, in retrospect, was probably this one: "Is there—is there any evidence that society in general gives substantial deference to the psychiatric profession in this respect?"

The answer, obviously, is yes. Though "mentally retarded" was a used in ordinary conversation, no intelligent person would claim that a layman's subjective judgment trumped the diagnosis of professionals. And unlike "insane," "intellectually disabled" was not a legal term with its own legal history. Thus it wasn't surprising that, when the case was decided on May 27, Kennedy enlisted professional definitions to help him protect intellectually disabled defendants like Hall. Joined by the four Democratic appointees, he voided the death sentence. "The Eighth Amendment's protection of dignity reflects the nation we have been, the nation we are, and the nation we aspire to be," he wrote. "This is to affirm that the nation's constant, unyielding purpose must be to transmit the Constitution so that its precepts and guarantees retain their meaning and force." Thus, "to impose the harshest of punishments on an intellectually disabled person violates his or her inherent dignity as a human being."

Florida's bright-line rule violated the amendment because "if the States were to have complete autonomy to define intellectual disability as they wished, the court's decision in *Atkins* could become a nullity, and the Eighth Amendment's protection of human dignity would not become a reality."

Kennedy quoted an amicus brief for the American Psychological Association arguing that the state's refusal to consider professional opinion "goes against the unanimous professional consensus." Intellectual disability was a medical condition, not a legal construct for courts or legislatures to redefine as they wished, he said.

"The death penalty is the gravest sentence our society may impose," he concluded. "Persons facing that most severe sanction must have a fair opportunity to show that the Constitution prohibits their execution. Florida's law contravenes our Nation's commitment to dignity and its duty to teach human decency as the mark of a civilized world. The States are laboratories for experimentation, but those experiments may not deny the basic dignity the Constitution protects."

In an angry dissent, Justice Alito wrote for his fellow Republican appointees that intellectual disability should be a legal category, defined democratically. "Under our modern Eighth Amendment cases, what counts are our society's standards—which is to say, the standards of the American people—not the standards of professional associations, which at best represent the views of a small professional elite," he argued. The courts were not obligated to follow these standards—which, after all, sometimes changed. And they weren't obligated to accept the statistical norms that came with IQ tests either. The test designers might *suggest* a "standard error of measurement," based on the results of repeated tests, but that figure didn't bind judges, who could make their own mathematical calculations of how reliable the tests were. In effect, a court could accept the test designers' *numerical score* but refuse to consider any information about *how it was derived.* "The appropriate confidence level is ultimately a judgment best left to legislatures," Alito concluded.

The majority opinion in *Hall* was almost a perfect capsule of the Kennedy approach. When his concept of dignity was at stake, he would throw the cloak of the Constitution over those in need. But to his conservative colleagues, his view of dignity meant little more than soft-headed dithering. Kennedy was not out of step with them—over the course of the term, his votes would go to the right on questions of campaign finance, union rights, and contraceptive care. But his methodology could hardly have been more different. He and his conservative colleagues agreed about the need to protect some groups—religious objectors to contraception or whites disadvantaged by affirmative action. They disagreed about protecting others, such as juveniles and the disabled. And their language was very different. Kennedy's diction, consciously poetic, drew less on contemporary conservative theory than on the gentle paternal diction of a small-town America that disappeared years ago.

Chapter 6

In a Different Voice

Justice Clarence Thomas

Susan B. Anthony List v. Driehaus

On Monday, February 24, 2014, the justices emerged from behind the velvet curtain to hear argument in an important regulatory case—*Utility Air Regulatory Group v. Environmental Protection Agency*, a challenge to the Environmental Protection Agency's authority to regulate greenhouse gas emissions. The justices peppered the lawyers with questions about the proper way to read a complex regulatory statute in light of changing definitions of "pollutants." Justice Breyer asked whether the Clean Air Act should be interpreted like "a statute that said you have to throw out all bubble gum that's been around for more than a month. Well, what about bubble gum used in a display case that nobody ever intends to eat?" Justice Scalia responded by asking, "Would you have to make an exception for bubble gum in the display window if the statute were subject to two interpretations, one of which would include display windows, and the other one of which wouldn't?" Analogies, metaphors, and dry intellectual ridicule ricocheted around the majestic courtroom as a capacity audience strained for a hint of which way the justices were leaning.

They learned nothing, however, from Justice Clarence Thomas. That Monday marked a melancholy anniversary for the court's sole African American member. It had now been eight full years since Thomas asked a question from the bench in a Supreme Court argument. The justice's voice is heard from the bench—he reads summaries of his own opinions for the court, as does every other justice, and in January 2013 he apparently made a joke at the expense of his alma mater, Yale Law School, that was inaudible to most in the courtroom. (The official transcript quotes him as saying only, "well . . . he did not . . ." apparently referring to a public defender in a criminal case.) But not since February 22, 2006 (when he asked a question about the legal standard for allowing evidence that another person has confessed to a crime for which a defendant is on trial) had he actually asked an advocate for a clarification, an explanation, or an elaboration.

The previous Friday, *New Yorker* legal correspondent Jeffrey Toobin, in an essay entitled "The Disgraceful Silence of Clarence Thomas," wrote that Thomas was refusing to listen to the arguments, simply "not paying attention." He added, "By refusing to acknowledge the advocates or his fellow justices, Thomas treats them all with disrespect. It would be one thing if Thomas's petulance reflected badly only on himself, which it did for the first few years of his ludicrous behavior. But at this point, eight years on, Thomas is demeaning the court." Toobin was being unfair. Those who sit in court day after day agree that Thomas is quite engaged, both with the case before him and with his colleagues on the bench. Sometimes his chair is tipped back to near invisibility. At other times, he eagerly leans forward to hear an advocate's answer; summons a page to bring him a volume of case law; or whispers, grinning broadly, to Stephen Breyer, the justice seated beside him.

Thomas is present in the courtroom. He simply will not speak.

His silence has many roots, though surely one lies in the controversy that almost cost him his seat on the court. In May 2013, just at the October 2012 term was winding down, documentary filmmaker Frieda Mock released a feature film entitled *Anita*. Marketed under the tagline "Speaking Truth to Power," the ninety-five-minute film included some of the rawest details of Thomas' confirmation hearings in October 1991. The Senate Judiciary Committee heard startling testimony from Anita Hill, an African American lawyer who (like Thomas) had graduated from Yale Law School. Hill had worked for Thomas when he was head of the Equal Employment Opportunity Commission. Hill told the panel that her boss had harassed her in the rawest possible terms, pressured her to view pornography, discussed his own genitalia and sexual prowess, and asked her repeatedly for sex. Supporters of Thomas fought back with a furious attack on Hill's truthfulness and sanity, while Thomas branded the committee's hearings "a high-tech lynching for uppity blacks."

Since his confirmation (by a vote of 52–48, it was the closest successful vote since the 1800s), Thomas has usually avoided comment on the controversy. But it has never died. Even Thomas's own wife, Virginia Lamp Thomas, found it impossible to let it go. *Anita* opened with audio of a bizarre phone call Virginia Thomas made to Hill's voice mail on October 9, 2010: "Good morning Anita Hill, it's Ginni Thomas. I just wanted to reach across the airwaves and the years and ask you to consider something. I would love you to consider an apology sometime and some full explanation of why you did what you did with my husband. So give it some thought. And certainly pray about this and hope that one day you will help us understand why you did what you did. OK, have a good day."

No one is quite sure what Ginni Thomas thought her call would accomplish, but it backfired badly on her and her husband. Stunned, Hill alerted the Federal Bureau of Investigation and released the audio to the public. Once again, the dispute between her and the justice was front-page news. Thomas made no comment on the phone call in 2010, or on the film three years later, or on the eighth anniversary of his silence in 2014.

Sitting on a bench populated by voluble, brilliant colleagues who thrive on attention, Thomas had managed to call attention to himself by saying nothing.

Thomas's career has taken him from deepest poverty to the summit of achievement and power. But his boyhood in the segregated South seems never to have left his mind. In fact, his most celebrated bench question was asked when an advocate seemed to him to be playing down the sheer terror of living under the South's Jim Crow racial dictatorship. In the 2002 case of *Virginia v. Black*, the government was defending a statute that made it a crime to burn a cross with the intent to intimidate another person. A government lawyer defended the statue as aimed at "threats of bodily harm."

Thomas interrupted, "Mr. Dreeben, aren't you understating the—the effects of—of the burning cross? . . . Now it's my understanding that we had almost one hundred years of lynching and activity in the South by the Knights of Camellia and—and the Ku Klux Klan, and this was a reign of terror and the cross was a symbol of that reign of terror. Was—isn't that significantly greater than intimidation or a threat?"

Appellate courts do not hear witnesses. But that question was vivid testimony. Thomas's voice summoned into the chamber a cloud of witnesses—African Americans who remembered racial segregation imposed by law and enforced by terror. Rodney A. Smolla, representing the cross-burning defendants, later wrote that the impact of the question was "palpable and physical." He added, "In all my life as an advocate and observer of legal proceedings, I have never seen the mood in a courtroom change so suddenly and dramatically."

Before the case, many commentators expected the court to strike down the Virginia statute. In fact, the court narrowed the statute to require direct proof of intent; the mere burning of a cross could not by itself prove that the defendant intended to intimidate. But the cross ban itself survived. (Thomas dissented from the court's requirement that the state separately prove intent to intimidate. To him, cross burning was not speech; it was crime in and of itself.)

In a recent e-mail, Smolla recalled a dinner with Thomas years later. "He looked at me, gave a great belly laugh, stabbed his finger in the air right at me, and cackled, 'I *got* you! I *got* you!' I laughed as hard as he did."

Thomas's voice may have changed history that day. He had spoken for many who could not speak for themselves. To listen to that argument audio is to understand what has been lost because Thomas has chosen to muzzle himself. That in itself is painful to think about. But for anyone with basic empathy, it's more painful to think of the wounds, the hesitations, the doubts, and the self-hatred that must underlie a refusal to play such a powerful role in the history of our time.

"I tend to be morose sometimes," Thomas told a group of high-school students in 2009. "There are some cases that will drive you to your knees."

For all his good humor—he trades broad smiles with colleagues and is revered by the court staff for his personal kindness and lack of pretension—Thomas does seem morose. Toobin was wrong to call his silence disgraceful, but it does seem profoundly sad. Though he does not speak in court, Thomas often appears before student and bar groups, and he is invariably asked about his silence. His explanations vary. The other justices, he says, already make it too hard for lawyers to make a point. (This court is certainly the "hottest bench" in history.) It is a courtesy to the advocates.

But beyond that, he is frank to admit it has personal roots. It is a wound that is very deep. And if his sadness seems odd to those who have not lived his life, that doesn't make it any less powerful.

Thomas was born in the tiny coastal town of Pin Point, Georgia. His father never featured in his life; his mother was so poor that, when Clarence was seven, she sent him to Savannah to be raised by his grandfather,

Myers Anderson, whom he ever afterward called "Daddy," "the greatest man I ever knew." He wrote in his memoir, *My Grandfather's Son*, that as a child he feared ridicule because he spoke Gullah, a Sea Island dialect of English that many people—black and white—find incomprehensible.

From first grade through college, Thomas was educated in Catholic schools. He seems to have felt fully accepted only at one—St. Benedict the Moor, the all-black grammar school he attended in Savannah. It was staffed by white nuns, he recalled, who "taught us that God made all men equal, that blacks were inherently equal to whites, and that segregation was morally wrong." When he entered mostly white schools, he encountered white racism for the first time. At first he trained for the Catholic priesthood, but his experiences at a seminary in Missouri convinced him that racism was endemic in the Church. When he told his grandfather he had changed his plans to seek ordination and instead wanted to attend Holy Cross College in Worcester, Massachusetts, his only paternal figure told him to leave home.

At Holy Cross and Yale Law School, he wrote, he was greeted with condescension—the barely concealed assumption that he was only present because white beneficence was tolerating his lack of preparation. In February 2014, he told students at Palm Beach Atlantic University that "the worst I have been treated was by northern liberal elites. The absolute worst I have ever been treated. The worst things that have been done to me, the worst things that have been said about me, by northern liberal elites, not by the people of Savannah, Georgia."

He told the Florida students,

My sadness is that we are probably today more race
and difference-conscious than I was in the 1960s when
I went to school. To my knowledge, I was the first
black kid in Savannah, Georgia, to go to a white school.
Rarely did the issue of race come up. Now name a day
it doesn't come up. Differences in race, differences in
sex, somebody doesn't look at you right, somebody
says something. Everybody is sensitive. If I had been
as sensitive as that in the 1960s, I'd still be in Savannah.
Every person in this room has endured a slight. Every
person. Somebody has said something that has hurt
their feelings or did something to them—left them out.
That's a part of the deal.

Thomas's memoir reveals that while he ignored the
slights he received, he never forgot them. When Sonia
Sotomayor was subjected to racist treatment by a law-
firm interviewer at Yale Law School, she complained so
intensely that the offending recruiter was required to
write a letter of apology in order to be allowed to return.
When law firm recruiters asked similar questions of
Thomas, he quietly withdrew his name from consideration. "I was among the elite," he concluded, "and I knew
that no amount of striving would make me one of them."

In OT13, Clarence Thomas was among the justices, but
twenty-two years had not made him one of them. Thomas
considered himself an "originalist" in constitutional questions. In that, of course, he echoed Scalia, the first avowed
"originalist" on the court. Yet the two men frequently interpreted constitutional provisions quite differently.

Their differences were vividly on display in the OT10 case, *Entertainment Merchants Association v. Brown*. A California statute made it a crime to sell a "violent video game" to a minor. Scalia, writing for six justices, held that the law violated the First Amendment. He looked back at the history of art and literature in the eighteenth century. Violence then was very much a part of protected expression, he wrote, for adults and for children. Given that history, there could not be a "violence" exception to free speech, like the historical exceptions for obscenity, conspiracy, fraud, and other types of "speech crime."

Thomas took an entirely different tack. "In my view," he wrote in dissent, "the 'practices and beliefs held by the founders' reveal another category of excluded speech: speech to minor children bypassing their parents." As evidence, he offered a 1648 statute of the Massachusetts colony that prescribing hanging for a "rebellious" son who "disobeyed 'the voice of his father, or the voice of his mother.'" It was an eccentric basis for interpreting twenty-first-century free speech doctrine—or even speech doctrine as of 1789.

The opinion highlighted another feature of Thomas's legal thought: he did not really care much for the court's own precedent when it conflicted with his own view of "original understanding." Scalia once told an interviewer that Thomas "does not believe in stare decisis, period." Scalia himself has said that stare decisis should count for something even in constitutional questions; in a comment that was seen as a slap at Thomas, he once said, "I am an originalist, but I am not a nut."

Thomas also tends not to be much interested in the narrow issue actually presented by facts of cases and lower-court decisions. In a high-profile federalism case, *Lopez v. United States*, the majority held that a federal statute banning guns in school zones was beyond the proper reach of Congress' power to "regulate commerce among the several states." The court's existing precedents, Chief Justice Rehnquist wrote, could not be stretched to cover laws that had "nothing to do with 'commerce' or any sort of economic enterprise." Thomas concurred, but he argued that the court should overturn a century of precedent and propound a rule defining "commerce" as "selling, buying, and bartering, as well as transporting for these purposes."

Thomas has said publicly that he drafts an opinion in outline form before hearing oral arguments; his view of a case is "almost never" changed at argument. He is notoriously unwilling to compromise his own views in order to win over his colleagues and often seems to prefer writing a sole dissent or concurrence reflecting his beliefs over writing a majority opinion that is ideologically impure.

Perhaps for that reason, Thomas is very seldom assigned to write high-profile constitutional opinions. The risk in such an assignment would be that Thomas would write language that would lose wavering votes and perhaps turn a win into a loss. In OT13, Thomas did get such an assignment in a First Amendment case called *Susan B. Anthony List v. Driehaus*. The issue at the heart of the case was this: can a state make it a crime to make a "false statement" about a candidate for political office during a campaign? The Susan B. Anthony List (SBA), an antiabortion PAC, charged in 2010 that Ohio Representative Steve Driehaus "voted for taxpayer-funded abortion" by supporting the Affordable Care Act. Driehaus complained to the state electoral commission, which found "probable cause" that SBA had violated the state's "false statement" law.

The commission scheduled a hearing for after the election; however, Driehaus was defeated for reelection, joined the Peace Corps, and dropped his complaint. SBA then asked a federal court to block future enforcement of the law because it wanted to campaign against other Democrats with the same charge. The lower courts dismissed the request because SBA was no longer in any jeopardy of being punished for its advertisement. The Court of Appeals noted that SBA insisted that its charge was true— that a vote for the ACA was a vote for "taxpayer-funded abortion." The majority bizarrely insisted that SBA would have standing to sue only if it admitted that it planned to lie.

The issue before the Supreme Court was thus narrow. Could the mere possibility of another complaint give SBA standing? If not, SBA argued, the statute could never be challenged—it was common for politicians to file complaints under the statute and then drop them after the votes were counted.

The law itself, most people agreed, was completely unconstitutional. Under the First Amendment, the state could not set itself up as an arbiter of truth and decide which political arguments were true and which were false. So shaky did the statute seem that Ohio's attorney general filed two briefs with the court—one on behalf of the commission supporting the law and the other on behalf of himself asking the court to overturn it.

Based on his historical disquisition in *Entertainment Merchants Association v. Brown*, one might think that Thomas would be inspired to set off into long discussions of the role of truth in the era of Blackstone; but in fact, *Susan B. Anthony List v. Driehaus* was restricted to the issue of "standing," and that wasn't hard. Thomas wrote for a unanimous court that SBA had standing. There is no clear "right to lie," but a lot of precedent—and simple common sense—to suggest that it's a bad idea to allow government officials to determine truth and threaten designated "liars" with incarceration. In fact, the existence of the law affects politics, even if no one is ever prosecuted; candidates can complain, get a "probable cause" ruling, and then proclaim that an opponent or critic has "lied."

In the unanimous opinion, Thomas wrote that "denying prompt judicial review would impose a substantial hardship on [SBA], forcing them to choose between refraining from core political speech on the one hand, or engaging in that speech and risking costly Commission proceedings and criminal prosecution on the other."

Thomas concluded that the law could not silence groups like SBA. Then he silenced himself once more.

Chapter 7

Bringer of Chaos

Justice Stephen Breyer

National Labor Relations Board v. Noel Canning

At a public appearance at the Georgetown Law Center in April 2014, Professor David Cole of Georgetown asked Justice Stephen G. Breyer a question about judicial method. "I am a bringer of chaos," Breyer replied, "and as a bringer of chaos I am not going to answer your question."

"Chaos" is not the word one would have most readily associated with Stephen Breyer. Both Breyer's manner and his writing exude a level of high culture unseen on the court since Oliver Wendell Holmes retired in 1932. For one thing, Breyer is a member by marriage of one of the noble houses of Britain—his father-in-law, John Hare, was Viscount Blakenham, son of the Earl of Listowel and son-in-law of Viscount Cowdray. Hare, who died in 1982, served for a time as the leader of Britain's Conservative

Party. Breyer also holds a first-class honors degree from Oxford University and is a former Harvard Law professor. From the bench, he has been known to ask a puzzled American lawyer a question based on the English game of cricket—"I think I have to say that you are on a weak wicket." In general, he is a product of dinner at a university high table and sherry in the senior common room.

He also demonstrates a familiarity with literature, art, and philosophy that are only slightly short of dazzling. His opinions bristle with references to Shakespeare and other canonical authors. At about the time that Justice Scalia was attracting notice with his "I believe in the devil" interview, Breyer was giving an interview of his own, in which he discussed at length his passion for French novelist Marcel Proust's seven-volume *À la recherche du temps perdu*. He had, he told the interviewer, read it not once but twice—in the original French. Breyer's confession brought him less notice than Scalia's; more Americans believe in Satan than have heard of Proust, and besides, Breyer's interview was given in French to the Paris-based literary monthly *Revue des Deux Mondes*.

Breyer's aristocratic pedigree actually goes back no further than the late 1950s. He was born in 1938 into a middle-class Jewish family in San Francisco. His father was a government lawyer and his mother was a community volunteer with political and civic groups. He graduated from a public high school there and got his undergraduate degree at Stanford. That degree, with highest honors, brought him a fellowship to Oxford and, later, admission to Harvard Law School. After law school, he alternated between government service—law clerk to Supreme Court Justice Arthur Goldberg, Justice Department lawyer, Watergate prosecutor, and finally chief counsel to the Senate Judiciary Committee—and the Harvard faculty, teaching courses on the complexities of the administrative process.

Proust, he told *Revue des Deux Mondes*, formed a part of his judges' tool kit: "When you're a judge and you spend your whole day in front of a computer screen, it's important to be able to imagine what other people's lives might be like, lives that your decisions will affect. People who are not only different from you, but also very different from each other. And this empathy, this ability to envision the practical consequences on one's contemporaries of a law or a legal decision, seems to me to a crucial quality in a judge."

But "empathy," like chaos, is not a word that jumps most immediately to mind at the mention of Stephen Breyer. In 1993, two Clinton administration lawyers wrote in a memo to the White House counsel that "there is very little heart and soul in Judge Breyer's opinions. Quite clearly, he is a rather cold fish." They had been evaluating Breyer for a Supreme Court nomination. The nomination went to Ruth Bader Ginsburg.

Yet there was clearly another side to Breyer's personality. In his service on Capitol Hill, he attracted fast friends among Republicans and Democrats, who found him thorough and fair-minded. Those bonds are responsible for his rise. President Jimmy Carter nominated Breyer to the Court of Appeals for the First Circuit nine days after the Republican landslide of 1980. It would have been easy for Senate Republicans to delay confirmation until the White House (and Senate majority) fell into their hands a few weeks later. But prodded by Utah Republican Orrin Hatch, the Republicans agreed to permit his confirmation.

A year after the nomination of Ginsburg, Clinton reached for Breyer. Clinton was politically weaker than he had been a year before; he needed someone with appeal across the aisle. Breyer was confirmed 87–9 and began service at the beginning of the October 1994 term.

"Cold fish" really is the wrong designation for Breyer. His enthusiasms are intellectual and complex, but they are deep. One Yale scholar, Paul Gewirtz, once wrote an essay entitled "The Pragmatic Passion of Stephen Breyer." It was a review of Breyer's 2005 book, *Active Liberty: Interpreting Our Democratic Constitution*, which laid out the justice's philosophy of judicial review. "Liberty," Breyer wrote, comes in two strands: "Modern liberty," an idea that flows from the Enlightenment, means the freedom from governmental restraint, the absence of government. "Ancient liberty," which arises out of classical Greek political theory, refers to the citizen's right to take part in government and be a part of the decisions that affect him or her.

The Constitution, Breyer argued, protects both. Individual rights by themselves are not enough; properly interpreted, the Constitution also sets up a democratic government, armed with power adequate to the challenges it faces, and opens its processes to participation by all.

The idea has deep roots—Breyer drew his notions of "ancient" and "modern" liberty from the nineteenth-century French-Swiss philosopher Benjamin Constant. It has, however, been obscured in the past half-century by the conservative insistence that government can never be a force for good. Reagan proclaimed that government was the problem, not the solution. Breyer does not believe that.

Breyer's book did not offer a theory of judging to match, say, Scalia's theory of "originalism." This is what he meant when he called himself a "bringer of chaos." Judging was not to be done on the basis of theory. A passionate pragmatist used traditional lawyers' tools—text, legislation, precedent, history, governmental structure, and above all practicality—to decide cases in ways that would further the aims of society. In a constitutional case, "original understanding" (whatever that might be) seemed to him less important than current understanding of how the provision had been adapted over the years to make our political system work; in a statutory question, the niceties of historical dictionaries seemed less important than resolving ambiguities in a way that furthered the statute's aims. The overwhelming concern was not the past but the future; not the antecedents of a rule but the consequences of a decision. Legal pragmatism, which first reached the Supreme Court in the person of Oliver Wendell Holmes, had deeper historical roots than Scalia's quest for "original understanding."

In the court's public sessions, Breyer cuts a remarkable figure. Slender and animated, with a high, gleaming forehead and mobile, slightly droopy features, he seems a bit like one of the famous engravings by Sir John Tenniel for the first edition of Lewis Carroll's *Alice* books, perhaps of the White Knight who produced so many strange devices for Alice, assuring her each time that "it's my own invention."

Breyer is always visibly engaged. He is also unfailingly polite. When, during an OT13 case, Justice Scalia humiliated an out-of-town lawyer for reading the beginning of his argument, Breyer cut off the spectacle to assure the poor wretch that he had done nothing wrong. At times he will trade a witticism with Clarence Thomas in the next seat over; at others he contorts himself into pretzel-like postures in his eagerness to grasp an advocate's forensic point. When he asks questions, perhaps as a result of his years as a law professor, he speaks slowly, proceeding by stages—checking from time to time to make sure the lawyer is following—and usually building his questions around quite elaborate hypotheticals. Combined with his cultured drawl, the result is a little like hearing a complex question of law posed by King Friday XIII on the old *Mr. Rogers' Neighborhood* children's television show.

Breyer's star OT13 turn came in a case called *National Labor Relations Board v. Noel Canning*. *Noel Canning*, one of the most-watched cases of the term, concerned an obscure presidential power called the "recess appointment." Article II of the Constitution provides that the president must obtain the "advice and consent" of the Senate before naming "ambassadors, other public ministers and consuls, judges of the Supreme Court, and all other officers of the United States." There's a narrow exception, however, in Article II, § 2, cl. 3: the president, acting alone, "shall have power to fill up all vacancies that may happen during the recess of the Senate, by granting commissions which shall expire at the end of their next session."

For more than two hundred years, presidents and senators have wondered what the words mean. First, does "happen during the recess of the Senate" limit the power to filling jobs that *become* vacant while the Senate is in recess? Second, does "the recess of the Senate" mean only the formal break between one yearlong formal "session" of the Senate and the next, or does it mean any time the body closes for business for more than a few days?

Beginning with George Washington, presidents have filled hundreds of vacancies by recess appointment. These include judgeships; both Chief Justice Earl Warren and Justice William J. Brennan were recess appointments by President Dwight Eisenhower. Recess appointees are usually but not always confirmed when the Senate returns. But relations between Congress and presidents have deteriorated in recent years. Once rare, filibusters against presidential nominations have become almost routine. Senators regularly block confirmation of a nominee, leading to standoffs that can last weeks, months, and even years.

In 2007, the Senate Democratic majority devised a stratagem to block President George W. Bush from using his recess power. When time came for a holiday break, the leadership declared that it would hold one-minute pro forma sessions. A single luckless senator was required to drive in from the DC suburbs every three days, gavel the empty chamber to order, and then adjourn. There would be no "recess" to trigger the power.

That 2007 dispute arose over Bush's plans to install conservative nominees at the National Labor Relations Board (NLRB), which is responsible for making sure that employers follow the law when dealing with labor unions. Democrats thought that the Bush appointees might favor management. When Barack Obama became president, Republicans feared his nominees would favor unions. Republicans filibustered them in turn. By early 2012, the NLRB was about to cease operations for lack of members.

The Senate Democrats in the majority did not have the votes to override the filibusters. They would have been glad to adjourn, clearing the way for Obama to use the power to appoint temporary NLRB members. But under Article I, § 5, cl. 4 of the Constitution, neither house can adjourn for more than three days "without the permission of the other." The Republican house refused the Democratic Senate permission to adjourn; so began the latest round of pro forma sessions.

Obama and his lawyers, however, announced that these were not real sessions—there was no quorum present and the Senate did not do any business. The Senate actually was in recess. The president named a full complement of members to the NLRB.

The NLRB issued a flurry of orders to employers, including one to a Yakima, Washington, soft-drink bottling plant, Noel Canning, Corp. The company sued. They argued that the NLRB was not validly appointed, making the order void.

In a panel dominated by conservatives, the Court of Appeals for the DC Circuit held for the company. The three-judge panel's opinion went far beyond the question of pro forma sessions. They held that because the clause used the words "*the* recess" of the Senate, there could only be one "recess" per yearlong session. That "intersession recess" had once lasted weeks or months as senators traveled back to their districts. Today, however, it lasts only a few minutes or hours at the end of the year. That would give the president the briefest of opportunities to make a recess appointment.

Not only must the *appointment* take place between sessions, the panel wrote, but the office itself must have *become vacant* during the brief interval between sessions. If an official resigned or died while the Senate was in session, the president could *never* make a recess appointment to that spot, even if the Senate later refused to consider the nomination and left town.

As a practical matter, the DC Circuit opinion read the recess appointment clause out of the Constitution; it seemed like nothing so much as a partisan slap at the Democratic president. The impression was stronger because all three of the panel's judges were appointees of Republican presidents. That was no coincidence: for four years, the Republican Senate minority had blocked confirmation of any Obama nominee to the DC Circuit. That guaranteed Republican dominance on the second-most powerful court in the country. The Circuit decides many important cases—like *Noel Canning*—about governmental structure and economic regulation. In addition, it is a training ground for future Supreme Court justices. Chief Justice Roberts and Justices Scalia, Thomas, and Ginsburg had all come to the Supreme Court from the DC Circuit.

The political heat surrounding *Noel Canning* was intense when the lower-court opinion appeared. The stakes, however, soon fell. In 2013, the reelected Obama negotiated an agreement with Senate Republicans, who soon confirmed a full complement of NLRB members. That November, the Senate's Democratic majority changed the rules to prohibit filibusters against most presidential nominees (ominously, the rules change did not cover future Supreme Court choices). By the time the case came to the Supreme Court in January 2014, the Senate was preparing to confirm a fourth Obama appointee to the DC Circuit, giving the Democratic appointees a crucial majority of active judges there. In most respects, then, the immediate significance of the case was over. The issue might flare up in the years ahead, however, if Republicans won control of the Senate in 2014 or after the election of a new president in 2016. So there was still drama when Solicitor General Donald Verrilli rose to argue that appointments during pro forma sessions were perfectly constitutional.

"Mr. Chief Justice, and may it please the court," Verrilli began. "The interpretation of the recess appointments clause that respondent urges would repudiate the constitutional legitimacy of thousands of appointments by presidents going back to George Washington, and going forward it would diminish presidential authority in a way that is flatly at odds with the constitutional structure the framers established."

There was little doubt where Scalia stood: "What do you do when there is a practice that flatly contradicts a clear text of the Constitution?" he asked Verrilli. "Which of the two prevails?"

Verrilli responded, "Now, I think the practice has to prevail, your honor." That answer did not please Scalia.

Breyer asked the solicitor general, "I can't find anything that says the purpose of this clause has anything at all to do with political fights between Congress and the president.... So what have I missed? Where is it in the history of this clause, in its origination, that it has as a purpose to allow the president to try to overcome political disagreement?"

"I don't think that's its purpose," Verrilli responded. "But it is in the Constitution." If the power is there, he implied, it can be used to make government work.

Breyer then asked Verrilli, "Give me another example in the Constitution where you have both language and purpose pointing one place and yet this court because of practice has come to the opposite conclusion."

Verrilli could not.

When the decision was announced in the last week of OT13, the result was 9–0; Obama's pro forma appointments were void. But the difference in reasoning, again, was huge. The majority opinion by Breyer (for himself, Kennedy, Ginsburg, Sotomayor, and Kagan) held that if the Senate says it's in session, then it is, and the president can't make any appointments. But, they added, the recess power is an important one; if the Senate does leave town, the president can make a temporary appointment, even if the "recess" is just an adjournment for ten days and even if the office was vacant before the recess began.

"The clause gives the president authority to make appointments during 'the recess of the Senate' so that the president can ensure the continued functioning of the federal government when the Senate is away," Breyer wrote; it should be read in accordance with that aim.

Scalia concurred in the result—but his was perhaps the first concurrence in the court's history to be read aloud from the bench like a dissent. Scalia angrily argued that the president can only make recess appointments in the brief (a few minutes, usually) annual gap between formal yearlong "sessions"; not only that, but he can only fill vacancies that also arise during those few minutes or hours. Now that the Senate can return at a moment's notice, he says, the recess clause "is, or rather, should be, an anachronism."

"Anachronism" was a curious term for an "originalist" to use. If the recess power could be discarded as "anachronistic," why not the "natural born citizen" requirement for the presidency or the "equal suffrage" requirement for the Senate? Scalia's opinion, in fact, seemed to be "living constitutionalism," inspired by contemporary libertarian theory rather than any reverence for "original understanding." The clause, like the rest of the Constitution, was *not* written to make government work, Scalia said. The Constitution was there to *block* government, indeed sometimes to paralyze it, not to empower it. Presidential inability to fill offices, like other forms of interbranch standoff, "is not a bug to be fixed by this court, but a calculated feature of the constitutional framework."

The opinions neatly framed the major philosophical divide within the court. Conservative ideology is increasingly dominated by the Reaganite's fear of government. Anything that weakens government is good. But to Breyer, a government that cannot function is not a sphere of active liberty. Citizens of an inert state are not citizens at all.

Chapter 8

The Alito Court

Justice Samuel Alito

Harris v. Quinn

In his 2011 book *Five Chiefs*, retired Justice John Paul Stevens questioned the custom of calling a period of the court's history by the name of its chief justice. Each new appointment to the court, Stevens argued, creates a new interpersonal dynamic and a new court. Thus, for example, he suggested, the current Roberts court should, since the ascension of Elena Kagan in 2010, be called the Kagan court. But a better name came into focus at the end of OT13. This was the Alito court.

No single appointment of the past generation had shifted the tone and jurisprudence of the court as decisively as the substitution of Alito for Sandra Day O'Connor in 2006. When she retired in 2006, O'Connor had been for nearly a generation the court's "swing vote," the center justice whose decision could not fully be predicted by her perceived partisan identity (Republican) or political philosophy (conservative). O'Connor was passionate about what she once called "the hard work of judging"— the process of matching precedents and legal principles to specific facts, often reaching a result that surprised and sometimes dismayed both onlookers and her colleagues. On occasion, she refused to toe the conservative line in areas like affirmative action and gay rights.

Nowhere did she disappoint conservatives more sharply than in an OT91 case called *Planned Parenthood of Southeast Pennsylvania v. Casey.* Conservatives had been waiting for a chance to overturn *Roe v. Wade* and return the issue of abortion to the states. In the single most dramatic decision of the term, however, O'Connor joined Kennedy and Justice David Souter to reaffirm *Roe's* "essential holding." That vote was, for a generation of legal conservatives, as bitter a betrayal as Roberts' vote in the health-care cases two decades later.

Casey loomed over the transition from O'Connor to Alito more than a decade later. The three justices had upheld most of a restrictive Pennsylvania law that imposed requirements like a twenty-four-hour waiting period and an "informed consent" provision. Under the "old" version of *Roe,* such measures would clearly have been struck down, but the plurality upheld them as a way for the state to demonstrate its "profound respect for unborn life."

One part of the law, however, did not pass the plurality's muster: a requirement that, in most cases, a pregnant married woman could not obtain an abortion without informing her husband of her intention to do so. The joint opinion's discussion of the notification issue was passionate, even splenetic, and few doubted that the voice was O'Connor's. "Women do not lose their constitutionally protected liberty when they marry," the joint opinion said. "A state may not give to a man the kind of dominion over his wife that parents exercise over their children."

The court below—the US Court of Appeals for the Third Circuit—had also struck down the "husband notification" provision as incompatible with *Roe*. One member of the panel, a young conservative appointed by President George H. W. Bush, had dissented, however. His opinion reasoned that the notification provision served a good purpose; it would impel women to hesitate about their abortion decision and then consult their husbands. "It seems safe to assume that some percentage, despite an initial inclination not to tell their husbands, would notify their husbands without suffering substantial ill effects," the dissent said. It was a paternalistic rationale. Women needed guidance in this decision and would probably be glad later that the state had forced them, for their own good, to reconsider.

On October 31, 2005, President George W. Bush unveiled his nominee to replace O'Connor: Samuel A. Alito of the Third Circuit, the author of that dissent. Times were changing on the court.

Once on the bench, Alito quickly made it clear that he was no Sandra Day O'Connor. There was no dithering, no "hard work of judging." Like a heavy item of cargo in a ship's hold, he quickly caused a noticeable list to the right.

He voted to uphold a federal partial-birth abortion ban, even though the ban contained no exception to protect the mother's health. He voted against affirmative action at any opportunity. He sided with the prosecution in almost every criminal prosecution. The Alito version of the First Amendment protected campaign donors, but he dissented in a case striking down a federal statute that made it a felony to sell videos of "animal cruelty," even if applied to films of legal dogfights. He dissented in a case holding that peaceful protest near a veteran's funeral was protected speech. He dissented bitterly in a case permitting a law school to deny recognition to a Christian group that excluded homosexuals or supporters of gay rights. Alito wrote angrily that the decision meant "no freedom for expression that offends prevailing standards of political correctness in our country's institutions of higher learning."

When Alito was named to the court, commentators had dubbed him "Scalito." But the two judges, though conservative, have different approaches. Scalia is an "originalist" and grounds his opinions in historical claims that the founding generation interpreted provisions the way he does (or would have, if they'd been asked). During his confirmation hearings, Alito made a similar claim: "In interpreting the Constitution, I think we should look to the text of the Constitution, and we should look to the meaning that someone would have taken from the text of the Constitution at the time of its adoption."

But once confirmed, Alito seemed less like "Scalito" than like a mirror image of Breyer. His decisions were based less on "original understanding" or precedent than on his horseback guess of which result would have better consequences.

During oral argument in an OT10 case, *Brown v. Entertainment Merchants Association*, the justices grappled with First Amendment protection for a new art form—video games. Scalia told the state's lawyer that he was "asking us to create a—a whole new prohibition which the American people never—never ratified when they ratified the First Amendment."

Alito interrupted, "I think what Justice Scalia wants to know is what James Madison thought about video games. Did he enjoy them?"

The jape embodied an important disagreement. In the eventual decision, Scalia, writing for five justices, struck down the law by citing the frequent depictions of violence in art and literature of the eighteenth century. Alito (joined by Roberts) concurred in the result only. The statute was unconstitutionally vague, he wrote—but the court should not assess video games as if they were colonial-era pamphlets illustrated with woodcuts. "We should not jump to the conclusion that new technology is fundamentally the same as some older thing with which we are familiar," he wrote. "There are reasons to suspect that the experience of playing violent video games just might be very different from reading a book, listening to the radio, or watching a movie or a television show."

In another case, *United States v. Jones*, Alito and Scalia again squared off on methodology. In *Jones*, federal agents, without a warrant, had attached a GPS tracker to a criminal suspect's car and then tracked his movements for a month. Plotting the suspect's movements showed them his "stash house," and he was arrested with large amounts of drugs. The government argued it did not need a warrant because merely tracking a car by GPS signal was not a "search" at all. The court unanimously disagreed. Writing for five justices, Scalia reached back into eighteenth-century British tort law—attaching *anything* to someone's property was a search. Alito (joined by Ginsburg, Breyer, and Kagan) argued instead that the case should be decided because of the emerging ability of computerized tracking to monitor every movement of every citizen, not on some rule of Augustan tort law. In the eighteenth century, government could not have tracked anyone for a month without "a gigantic coach, a very tiny constable, or both—not to mention a constable with incredible fortitude and patience," Alito wrote.

As a justice, Samuel Alito looks forward, not back.

Since his student days, when he organized a conference on "The Boundaries of Privacy in American Society," Alito had worried about the potential of new technology to hurtle American into a pitiless dystopia, and he believed that the court should do what it could to forestall that. However, Alito would usually side with institutions over individuals. The criminal justice system, including prisons, should make few concessions to individual rights. Corporations and employers needed protection from greedy employees, not the other way around.

And, finally, Alito as a judge is deeply emotional. Writing in the *New York Times* in 2011, Emily Bazelon noted that "Alito has proved himself to be the closest thing conservatives have to a feelings justice." In vivid language, Alito could write of the anguish of a father facing protesters at a son's funeral or of Italian American job applicants denied a civil-service promotion. But, she noted, "Alito expresses feelings mostly for people who are a lot like him." And he can write with acid scorn of those with whom he does not empathize—civil rights plaintiffs, for example, or prison inmates.

On the bench, too, Alito's style is emotional and unguarded. Mark Joseph Stern of *Slate* wrote the following in 2013:

> Alito has long stood out as the rudest, most impudent justice, broadcasting his hostility and impatience to advocates and colleagues alike. He treats lawyers like children caught in a lie, grilling them on every minor point of their argument while dismissing their logic as idiotic. He handles fellow justices like hecklers who have thoughtlessly interrupted his train of thought. His demeanor is one of gruff agitation; he constantly sounds like he would rather be somewhere else. . . . On the bench, he tramples advocates' arguments with a dismissive sneer and openly cuts down his colleagues' logic.

His contempt for those who disagree was on full display in the last two cases of OT13, both delivered from the bench by Samuel Alito. That moment signaled the maturity of the Alito court and its namesake. These were the most-watched cases of the end of term. They were highly political. They were decided according to rigidly conservative principles and written in take-no-prisoners style.

There was a new sheriff in town.

The first of Alito's two opinions was *Harris v. Quinn*. *Harris* was a case close to the heart of the Republican Party because it had the potential to cripple one of the party's most persistent and successful enemies—the unions that represented public workers.

In states where public-employee unions were permitted to organize and bargain, they were usually required by law to represent all workers—not just their members.

Some states permitted the union to charge nonmembers an "agency fee" that paid it for its work in negotiating. For First Amendment reasons, the agency fee had to exclude any costs of political activity, litigation, and lobbying the legislature; if it did not, the exclusive representation provisions and the agency fees would violate the nonmembers' First Amendment rights. But a long line of Supreme Court precedent (named after a case called *Abood*) had repeatedly held that there was no violation as long as the payments are for bargaining and grievance services only. The cases reasoned that the unions played an important part in keeping "labor peace" in public workplaces and also in communicating workers' concerns to management effectively; this service to both workers and state justified any burden on nonmembers' free-speech rights. If the nonmembers did not pay a fee, they would be "free riders," benefiting from union efforts on their behalf but not carrying a share of the costs.

Harris v. Quinn concerned the application of these principles to a new kind of worker—in-home health-care workers. A joint state and federal program (Medicaid picks up much of the tab) provides care to elderly and disabled clients in their homes. Without in-home help, these patients would have to go into nursing homes. The arrangement preserves their dignity and autonomy and is much cheaper than nursing home care.

The health-care workers are selected by the recipients themselves. The state then approves them, provides training, and pays their salaries.

In 2003, twenty thousand in-home health-care workers in Illinois's Rehabilitation Program voted to choose the Service Employees International Union as their "bargaining representative." Illinois state law allowed the union a "fair share" fee. A number of Rehabilitation Program workers objected to the fees and, represented by lawyers from the National Right to Work Legal Defense Foundation, challenged the fees as a violation of their First Amendment rights.

In an OT11 case, *Knox v. Service Employees International Union*, the court's conservative majority suggested it was ready to reach back forty years and overturn *Abood*. In *Knox*, Alito, quoting an earlier case, wrote that "compulsory fees constitute a form of compelled speech and association that imposes a 'significant impingement on First Amendment rights.' . . . Our cases to date have tolerated this 'impingement,' and we do not revisit today whether the court's former cases have given adequate recognition to the critical First Amendment rights at stake."

The "tolerated" language seemed to many like a signal that the majority would like to clip the wings of public-employee unions. The challenge to the Illinois program was quickly forthcoming. At oral argument in January, William Messenger of the National Right to Work Legal Defense Foundation asked the court to overturn *Abood* and abolish the "agency fee" nationwide. "This is—I'm just going to use the word here, it is a radical argument," Kagan told him from the bench. "It would radically restructure the way workplaces across this country are—are run." Since 1948, she pointed out, states have had the power to enact "right-to-work" laws that limit union power. The states with agency fees chose to follow a different path. Was Messenger arguing that "a right-to-work law is constitutionally compelled"?

"In the public sector, yes," he replied.

Alito made clear at oral argument that, in his view, public-employee unions are nothing but a political boondoggle. "Governor Blagojevich got a huge campaign contribution from the union and virtually as soon as he got into office he took out his pen and signed an executive order that had the effect of putting, what was it, $3.6 million into the union coffers?" he asked the attorney for the union. She responded that, after the executive order, the legislature had ratified it by statute.

"You're asking us to overturn a case that's been the law for thirty-five years," Justice Stephen Breyer told Messenger. If the court overruled *Abood*, he said, the result would be endless litigation. "The courts of the United States are going to fashion, using the First Amendment as their weapon, a new special labor law for government employees."

The unions' best hope seemed to be Scalia. In a 1991 case called *Lehnert v. Ferris Faculty Association*, he had written this summary of the "free rider" argument: nonmembers of unions "are free riders whom the law requires the union to carry—indeed, requires the union to go out of its way to benefit, even at the expense of its other interests." Free ridership was "mandated by government decree," he wrote, and that might justify any burden on nonmembers' First Amendment rights.

Court watchers speculated that Scalia might stand by his earlier words, perhaps supported by Roberts or Kennedy, to save the union. But when the last day came, Justice Scalia did not even appear on the bench. The chief justices' opening words were, "Justice Alito has two opinions today." Beyond announcing the new importance of

Samuel Alito, the only question was how grievous a defeat the labor movement would suffer at his hands.

Alito seemed to burn with desire to overturn *Abood*, but he did not. The heart of the opinion—fully one-third of its thirty-nine pages—was devoted to attacking *Abood* as wrongly decided.

Instead, his opinion concluded that the home health-care workers were not "full-fledged" state workers and thus *Abood* did not apply to them. To apply that case to the home health-care workers would be an "extension" of *Abood*, and since *Abood* was wrong, Alito said, the court would decline to do that. Alito, and some if not all the other four justices who signed on to the opinion, were begging groups like Messenger's to bring a case involving real "full-fledged" public employees so that they could put a stake through *Abood*'s heart.

Any collective bargaining in the public sector, Alito wrote, is inherently political. Thus "agency fees" are not payment for negotiation but money extorted in order to subsidize political activity the worker may not support. "Speech by a powerful union that relates to the subject of Medicaid funding cannot be equated with the sort of speech that our cases have treated as concerning matters of only private concern," he wrote. It was the equivalent of forcing innocent citizens to recite pledges of political loyalty they did not truly believe in.

The opinion dismissed the idea that a union did the home health-care workers any good at all. Even if some workers need unions, these people, he suggested, don't. He cited a provision of federal National Labor Relations Act that denies union rights to "any individual employed . . . in the domestic service of any family or person at his home."

This, he said, showed that "the organization of household workers like the personal assistants does not further the interest of labor peace."

Alito did not say—indeed, he may not have known—that the "domestic service" exemption of the federal act, like the similar exemption of agricultural workers, was put there to protect Southern segregation from federal interference. In a 1993 article, scholars Ira Katznelson, Kim Geiger, and Daniel Kryder wrote, "The bill's crafters designed these exemptions to keep the majority of the African American workforce unorganized and exploited."

As Alito had devoted his energy to attacking *Abood*, Elena Kagan, in her dissent, strove to reaffirm it. "One aspect of today's opinion is cause for satisfaction, though hardly applause," she wrote. "As this case came to us, the principal question it presented was whether to overrule *Abood*. . . . Today's majority cannot resist taking potshots at *Abood*, but it ignores the petitioners' invitation to depart from principles of *state decisis*."

The doctrine of stare decisis requires the court to follow its own precedent unless some special circumstances have made it obsolete. The aim of Kagan's dissent seemed to be to shame a future majority out of overturning *Abood*. She concluded, "For some 40 years, *Abood* has struck a stable balance" in the public-employee context. "The balance *Abood* struck thus should have defeated the petitioners' demand to invalidate Illinois's fair-share agreement."

The *Harris* opinion was bad news for organized labor, and it seemed to warn of more bad news to come. If all public employee bargaining, even over wages, is political, then all public-employee union fees, and possibly all public-employee unions themselves, violate the First Amendment. The logic of much of Alito's opinion would apply to "full-fledged" state workers as readily as to home health-care workers.

Alito had warned the unions twice. The sheriff was on their trail.

Chapter 9

No Exit

Justice Ruth Bader Ginsburg

Dissenting, Burwell v. Hobby Lobby Stores

In October 2013, Ruth Bader Ginsburg was eighty. She was a double survivor of cancer—colon cancer in 1999 and pancreatic cancer, or a precursor to it, in 2009. Martin Ginsburg, her husband of fifty-six years, had died on a Sunday in June 2010. By all accounts, Ruth and Marty Ginsburg had an exceptionally close and happy marriage. Ruth Ginsburg was on the bench the following day.

In the fall of 2013, Ginsburg told Adam Liptak of the *New York Times* that she intended to remain on the bench "as long as I can do the job full steam, and that, at my age, is not predictable." Commentators suggested that she had a duty to resign in order to give a Democratic president a chance to fill her spot. "There will be a president after this one, and I'm hopeful that that president will be a fine president," she said.

Washington Post reporter Robert Barnes traveled with Ginsburg on her annual family vacation that summer. His profile was entitled "The Question Facing Ruth Ginsburg: Stay or Go?" The story described Ginsburg hiking in the Sangre de Cristo mountains; Ginsburg indulging her passion for opera under the stars; Ginsburg enjoying epic meals with friends, including "Winnie Klotz, a former dancer and for decades the photographer for the Metropolitan Opera," who "startles the gathering by grabbing her eighty-four-year-old ankle and lifting it straight above her eighty-four-year-old head."

Barnes's article appeared on October 4, the day before OT13 began. Just as Justice Scalia had sent a message with his carefully timed talk of the devil, Ginsburg was letting the world, and her colleagues, know that reports of her impending resignation were grossly exaggerated.

The calls continued. In February, retired Representative Barney Frank, a liberal icon and the first openly gay member of Congress, told an interviewer that "she should follow the example of Sandra Day O'Connor," who had resigned while her party held the White House. In March, Erwin Chemerinsky, one of the most prominent constitutional scholars in the country, wasted no words in a *Los Angeles Times* op-ed: "Justice Ruth Bader Ginsburg should retire from the Supreme Court after the completion of the current term in June. . . . Only by resigning this summer can she ensure that a Democratic president will be able to choose a successor who shares her views and values." But by May, as the term was winding down, she told Jess Bravin of the *Wall Street Journal*, "I can't say that I ignore [the clamor], but I have to do what seems to me to be right." For now, that was to stay.

Male demands that she get out of the way had never influenced Ruth Ginsburg much. When she was a first-year law student, the legendary Erwin Griswold—who spent two decades terrifying students as dean of Harvard Law School and was later US solicitor general—asked Ginsburg what she could possibly accomplish as a lawyer that would justify her taking up a spot that could go to a man. Ginsburg hadn't flinched. Barney Frank probably didn't compare.

Beyond that, Ginsburg was not on the court because of the benevolence of the Democratic Party. Of the eight other justices on the Roberts court in OT13, six—Roberts, Scalia, Thomas, Breyer, Alito, and Kagan—had risen in their careers thanks to a party and a president. Ginsburg made her way up on the outside as an upstart who challenged the men who named judges. She has expressed admiration for Barack Obama, but it was hard to imagine that she thought of him as her leader. And she seemed to be calculating that the next president would be a Democrat. ("I think it's going to be another Democratic president [in 2016]," she told Barnes.) Left unsaid was the possibility that it would be not just "a" Democrat but a specific one—Hillary Rodham Clinton, who would be the country's first female president. Handing Clinton a first-term nomination might seem more satisfying, and even better judicial politics, than subjecting the already weakened Obama to a bruising confirmation fight in the waning years of his second term. Obama, faced with Republican intransigence, might be compelled to choose a bland, centrist nominee. Ruth Ginsburg was no flaming liberal, but she wasn't bland.

Only three years before, at the end of OT09, Ginsburg had picked up a new and very important role. With the retirement of John Paul Stevens in June 2010, she became the senior moderate-liberal justice. By custom, in any case where the court is split, the senior dissenting justice assigns one justice to write the principal dissent. This meant that, in a high-profile ideological case, Ginsburg would have the task of leading the moderate-liberal bloc and, if necessary, writing the dissent herself.

On Monday, June 30, the last day of OT13, Ginsburg exercised that role in a dissent she read from the bench. The case was *Burwell v. Hobby Lobby Stores*. She was disagreeing directly with her junior colleague Samuel Alito, who sat to her immediate left. On the last occasion when this happened, Alito had showed elaborate scorn during Ginsburg's dissent, shaking his head, rolling his eyes, and mouthing the word "no" as she spoke. The public commentary on his rudeness had been harsh. On June 30, Alito maintained a stone face while Ginsburg read.

The first words of her oral dissent laid out her vision of the case and the stakes: "Under the Affordable Care Act, employers with health plans must provide women with access to contraceptives at no cost. The court holds today that commercial enterprises, employing workers of diverse faiths, can opt out of contraceptive coverage if contraceptive use is incompatible with the employers' religious beliefs."

The ACA requires large employers either to pay a tax or to provide health insurance for their employees. The health insurance provided must comply with guidelines developed for the Department of Health and Human Services (HHS) by the Institute of Medicine. The act required

HHS to develop guidelines for preventive care: the final guidelines required coverage for vaccination, diabetes screenings, domestic-violence counseling, and the full set of medically approved contraceptive methods. Businesses that have fifty or fewer employees did not need to provide the insurance or pay the tax. "Religious employers," such as churches and convents, could omit contraceptive coverage from their plans altogether. Religiously *affiliated* nonprofits, such as hospitals, were allowed to certify their objection to contraception; their employees would receive coverage from the third-party insurer without participation by the employer.

Hobby Lobby Stores and Conestoga Wood, however, don't fit any of these categories. They are for-profit corporations. Conestoga Wood, owned by a Mennonite family, makes specialty wood products and employs 950 people; Hobby Lobby is a chain of craft stores owned by devout Baptists, with 13,000 full-time employees. Both families object to four currently approved methods of contraception, claiming they are "abortifacients."

They brought suit demanding an exemption permitting them to offer policies to employees that would not cover those four methods. Their claim was based on the Religious Freedom Restoration Act (RFRA). That statute had been passed to correct one of the Rehnquist court's least popular decisions. In 1990, the court held that the state of Oregon could deny unemployment insurance to Galen Black, a white man, and Al Smith, a Klamath Indian. The two had been fired for attending a peyote ceremony conducted by an offshoot of the Native American Church. Before this case, known as *Employment Division v. Smith*, the court had, time and again, upheld the right of religious dissenters to unemployment compensation. This case, Justice Scalia argued, was different. The two men had violated a criminal law, he suggested (even though the state had never charged them with any crime). The free exercise clause, Justice Scalia wrote for the court, provided no shelter for individual religious acts that are forbidden by "neutral, generally applicable" laws.

The decision had outraged both civil libertarians and religious groups. RFRA had been passed in response; its aim was to restore the "compelling interest" test from the court's previous religious-freedom cases—the state may not "substantially burden" a "person's" practice of religion unless there is a "compelling interest" and the burden is the "least restrictive means" to further it.

In *Hobby Lobby*, the companies faced a series of obstacles: no previous case had ever held that a for-profit corporation—unlike churches and religious nonprofits—could have a "religion" or "exercise" it. Next, did the "mandate" really "burden" the corporations' "free exercise of religion" at all? Neither any of the individual stockholders nor the corporation itself would provide contraception directly to the women; the women decided, independently of their employer, what if any contraception they would use and then billed their health insurer for the cost.

Even if the companies had "free exercise rights," and even if the mandate was a "substantial burden," the act permits government to enforce it if it is the "least restrictive means" of achieving a "compelling governmental interest." Were the act's aims—expanding health-care coverage for workers and families, boosting public health generally, and facilitating women's access to reproductive health in particular—"compelling"? The companies argued that if the interest was really "compelling," the act would contain no exceptions at all. Since small for-profit companies were exempt, large ones should also be exempt. And if some form of exemption was tolerable, then the mandate directed at the companies could not be "the least restrictive means."

Oral argument in March was perhaps the hottest ticket of the term. Not only was the issue explosive, but conservative superlawyer Paul Clement was arguing for the companies. Clement, who had argued most of the challenge to the ACA in 2012, was clearly a favorite of the justices by reason of his clarity, humility, and quickness on his feet. In his argument, he dismissed the idea that the contraceptive requirement furthered any "compelling interest." "When the government pursues compelling interest, it demands immediate compliance," he said. "It doesn't say, 'Get around to it whenever it's convenient.' I can't imagine Congress passing Title VII [of the Civil Rights Act of 1964, which forbids employment discrimination by race, religion, sex, and national origin] and saying, 'Stop discriminating on the basis of race, unless of course you have a preexisting policy that discriminates on the basis of race, and then you can keep it as long as you'd like.'"

Actually, Kagan pointed out, Title VII had done the exact thing Clement claimed it had not: when passed, the statute delayed its nondiscrimination rule for small businesses in order to give the owners time to adjust to a new workplace and new rules. Solicitor General Donald Verrilli also reminded the court that, a half-century after passage, Title VII still doesn't apply to very small employers—those with fewer than fifteen employees. The Americans with Disabilities Act had also delayed its prohibition on disability discrimination for two full years to allow time to prepare, Verrilli said. Would Clement suggest that blocking disability discrimination was not a "compelling interest"? "I don't think anybody would doubt that the Americans with Disabilities Act advances interest of the highest order," Verrilli said.

In fact, Verrilli said, the contraceptive requirement's exemptions were few and narrow. Employees of churches and so on would not be covered—but employees of religiously affiliated nonprofits will get their coverage from the insurer when their employer certifies its objection to paying.

In an exchange that would later loom large, Clement suggested the government could use the same method to accommodate his clients. Sotomayor tried to pin him down: "You're saying they would claim an exemption like the churches have already?"

Clement dodged, "We haven't been offered that accommodation."

Justice Kennedy seemed troubled that Clement ignored the interests of the corporations' employees: "The employee may not agree with these religious—religious beliefs of the employer. Does the religious beliefs just trump? Is that the way it works?"

"Yes," Clement answered.

Clement's answer may have troubled Kennedy, but an answer of Verrilli's may have troubled him even more. Kennedy asked him whether "a profit corporation could be forced . . . in principle to pay for abortions."

Verrilli responded, "If it were for a for-profit corporation and if such a law like that were enacted, then you're right, under our theory . . . the for-profit corporation wouldn't have an ability to sue [under RFRA]."

On the last day of the term, Alito had already delivered one conservative victory in *Harris v. Quinn*. Most observers had expected him to write that one. His designation as author of *Hobby Lobby*, however, was surprising. His views on abortion and the ACA were well known, and they were strong.

The conundrum of the "contraceptive mandate" involved two sets of consciences. On one side were the employers, whose Christian faith convinced them that four methods of contraception took human life in violation of God's law, but on the other side were thousands of Hobby Lobby employees. The spiritual questions surrounding contraception and abortion were, to many on both sides of that line, issues for their own faith and conscience; giving an employer a potential veto on their decision might compromise the employees' religious freedom—and even their equality as human beings, since no medical services for men were being blocked by religious employers.

In Alito's opinion, however, only one set of consciences, one group of people, mattered. Female employees—women who might need contraception for family planning or other health reasons—were not even of secondary interest. His opinion barely mentioned them or their concerns.

Alito introduced the families—the Greens and the Hahns—as plucky American entrepreneurs. Their companies were incorporated, of course, making them legal "persons" separate from their stockholders. But that was of no consequence. The court never held that for-profit corporations had rights under the act or the religion clauses—but it never held they didn't. "The purpose of [the corporate personhood] fiction is to provide protection for human beings," he wrote. A victory for the companies would "protect the religious liberty of the humans who own and control these companies."

Denying the companies religious exemptions to the mandate would be unconscionable religious discrimination against the families. The government "would put these merchants to a difficult choice: either give up the right to seek judicial protection of their religious liberty or forgo the benefits . . . of operating as corporations."

On first reading, the opinion seemed to be limited to what are called "closely held" corporations, in which the stock is not freely traded and shareholders are often members of the same family. That would have been less of a limit than it sounds, since, as Hobby Lobby itself demonstrates, such corporations can become huge employers. But on close reading, Alito's opinion didn't say that large, publicly traded companies could not claim the protection of RFRA. In fact, it more or less explicitly said that they could—though, in soothing tones, Alito wrote that "it seems unlikely" that "corporate giants . . . will often assert RFRA claims."

The "burden" on the two families was "substantial," not reduced at all just because the decision to use contraception would be made by individual employees without the participation of the employer. The plaintiffs believed that allowing employees to make that independent decision made the company and its shareholders complicit in sin; for the court to deny their pain, Alito wrote, would "in effect tell the plaintiffs that their beliefs are flawed."

The corporation could avoid involvement by dropping insurance coverage altogether. This would trigger a $2,000 per employee tax—an amount comparable to, and probably less than, the cost of insuring that employee. But this would still violate the stockholders' religious rights, because the families "have religious reasons for providing health-insurance coverage for their employees." This meant, in effect, that a corporation had a religious right to require its employees to accept only such insurance as their employers deemed appropriate. As Clement had suggested, the burden on employees' religious rights was irrelevant.

The government claimed a "compelling interest" in "very broad terms, such as promoting 'public health' and 'gender equality,'" Alito wrote. The scare quotes implied skepticism about the importance of these interests, but the opinion glided over this question, stating that "we will assume" such an interest in providing contraception to female employees. The government, however, had not shown that the mandate was the "least restrictive means" of achieving its goals.

In the opinion's most startling passage, Alito suggested that contraception shouldn't be required in ACA health plans at all. If the government believed contraception was so important, Alito wrote, why did it not just "assume the cost of providing the four contraceptives at issue to any women who are unable to obtain them under their health-insurance policies"? Compared to the overall cost of the ACA, Alito wrote, a few hundred million dollars more did not seem all that consequential.

This was a startling idea—that there was something special about contraception that barred health programs from requiring it. It seemed like a somewhat stilted statement of something right-wing talk-radio hosts had been saying for months: why should employers have to pay for their female employees' contraceptive choices? This wasn't a health requirement at all, the far right had insisted, but a compelled subsidy of immoral sexual choices like abortion or promiscuity. Given Alito's skepticism about the health rationale behind the contraceptive rule, he seemed to have adopted an extreme, and arguably misogynistic, reading of the record.

If the government wouldn't pay for the contraceptives itself, Alito continued, then why shouldn't it just offer the for-profit companies the same "accommodation" it had offered religious nonprofits? All such bodies—hospitals or charities, for example—had to do was certify to HHS that they objected to providing contraceptive benefits; the act then required the insurers to provide the benefits to the employees at no "net cost" to either employees or employers.

It seemed like legal statesmanship—an easy solution to a hard moral problem. The suggestion, however, was less solid than it seemed. First, the religious nonprofits themselves had already rejected the "accommodation" and were suing in lower courts to block it. Second, when Sotomayor at oral argument had asked Clement whether the accommodation would satisfy his clients, the lawyer had refused to answer. Third and finally, Alito's opinion made clear that the court today "did not decide whether an approach of this type complies with RFRA." The government might offer the concession; but the issue would end up in front of the Court again, and the majority might reject the accommodation as well.

Some of the language in the majority opinion was so sweeping that Kennedy apparently felt compelled to soften it in a four-page concurrence, not read from the bench. First, despite the scare quotes in Alito's opinion, Kennedy wanted to "confirm that a premise of the court's opinion is its assumption that [the mandate] furthers a legitimate and compelling interest in the health of female employees." Second, Alito's suggestion that government might need to directly fund all contraception had plainly alarmed him. Kennedy at least was not willing to agree that, if the "accommodation" failed, the only solution would be "for the government to create an additional program." If claimants rejected the accommodation, he suggested, his vote might be up for grabs in a later case.

After the majority had its say, Ginsburg dissented aloud. Her opinion was joined by the four Democratic appointees, but its rhetoric left little doubt that she was seeking to give a voice to thousands of female workers around the country. The majority, she wrote, held that "RFRA demands accommodation of a for-profit corporation's religious beliefs no matter the impact that accommodation may have on their parties who do not share the corporations' owners' religious faith—in these cases, thousands of women employed by Hobby Lobby and Conestoga."

She quoted the court's previous abortion decisions to illustrate the harm that Hobby Lobby and other religious employers wanted to inflict on their female workers: "The ability of women to participate equally in the economic and social life of the nation has been facilitated by their ability to control their reproductive care." Over the next six pages, she outlined the specifics behind the "public health and gender equality" interests the majority had found insubstantial. Economic and medical studies showed "the disproportionate burden women carried for comprehensive health services and the adverse health consequences of excluding contraception" from their benefits. Pregnancy carried fatal risks for women with "some congenital heart diseases, pulmonary hypertension, and Marfan syndrome." Contraceptives were also used to forestall endometrial cancers and other serious health conditions. Unintended pregnancies often produced depression in the mothers and premature birth in the babies.

The majority was ignoring these burdens even though previous cases held that religious accommodations "must not significantly impinge on the interests of third parties." Its claim that RFRA covered for-profit companies was "not plausible" given that both the constitutional case law before RFRA's passage and the record of its adoption showed no discussion of the issue. The claim that RFRA protected a corporation against any "involvement" in contraceptive-providing health insurance also mocked the autonomy of the women who would make the actual choices. "Any decision to use contraceptives made by a woman covered under Hobby Lobby's or Conestoga's plan will not be propelled by the government," Ginsburg wrote. "It will be the woman's autonomous choice."

The court's supposed solution was improper, she wrote: a "'least restrictive means' cannot require employees to relinquish benefits accorded them by federal law in order to ensure that their commercial employers can adhere unreservedly to their religious tenets."

Beyond that, the majority opinion was not narrow; it was one "of startling breadth," Ginsburg wrote. "Although the court attempts to cabin its language to closely held corporations, its logic extends to corporations of any size, public or private" who were now likely to seek "religion-based exemptions from regulations they deem offensive to their faith." Moreover, drawing on actual case law, she noted that commercial enterprises had in the past sought religious exemptions from laws against excluding nonwhites from public restaurants and hiring single women working without their fathers' consent. Companies had already brought suits in lower courts demanding exemption from paying premiums for *any* method of contraception. Future challenges might to involve refusal to facilitate blood transfusions, antidepressants, and vaccinations.

The majority could not repel the next wave of claims without picking and choosing among its favorite beliefs. "The court, I fear, has ventured into a minefield," she wrote.

At the end of her oral statement, Ginsburg added these words: "Our cosmopolitan nation is made up of people of almost every conceivable religious preference. In passing RFRA, Congress did not alter a tradition in which one person's right to free exercise of her religion must be kept in harmony with the rights of her fellow citizens, and with the common good."

Aside from the chief justice's ceremonial words adjourning court until October, those were the last words spoken in OT13. There was nothing valedictory in their tone. As the justices rose to depart, Alito politely stood aside while the frail form of his antagonist slowly slipped out of sight behind the curtain.

Epilogue

Justice in Red and Blue

For a few days toward the end of OT13, observers and journalists had whispered about a surprising possibility. What if the term ended not with a bang but with a smile? There had been a remarkable stretch of cases decided by 9–0 votes. In some cases that seemed contentious, one of the conservative majority made common cause with the moderate liberals to produce a narrow result. Thus, in *Noel Canning*, Kennedy voted for Breyer's narrow opinion, preserving at least the possibility of "recess appointments" in a future emergency. In a case called *McCullen v. Coakley*, the court voted 9–0 to invalidate a Massachusetts statute providing a thirty-five-foot "buffer zone" around abortion clinics, where no one but patients and clinic employees could gather. Roberts crossed that time to support a narrow result; the four conservatives wanted a rule that would have made any "buffer zone" a gross violation of the First Amendment. The chief's opinion carefully rejected that reasoning and refused to overturn earlier cases approving buffer zones; instead, he agreed with the four Democratic appointees that a thirty-five-foot zone was too big.

In *Bond v. United States*, conservatives had pursued a cherished goal: cutting back on the federal government's power to make treaties with other countries, possibly permitting states to block environmental or human-rights treaties. Roberts took the lead in that case, too. Writing for six justices, he overturned the rather absurd conviction of a jilted wife who smeared toxic chemicals on her rival's mailbox. Such an ordinary crime could not be punished as use of "chemical weapons," forbidden under an international treaty. But his opinion took nothing away from the power itself, and three conservatives—Scalia, Thomas, and Alito—concurred but denounced this missed opportunity.

And in a case called *Riley v. California*, the chief had written for a truly unanimous court that police could not search through the data on cell phones without a warrant, even when they had legally arrested the owners. It was a popular decision, written with his characteristic flair, and it drew praise across the political and legal spectrum.

Perhaps something really was changing inside the court. Even if the last two decisions were split (as most expected they would be), the court's percentage of unanimous results was sharply up, the number of 5–4 decisions lower than usual. The chief justice might have succeeded in building his commitment to unanimity and in moving the court away from the bitterest of partisan disputes.

But on June 30, Roberts's first words were, "Justice Alito has two opinions today."

OT13 ended with a snarl.

In fact, the clerk's final gavel on June 30 did not signal even a momentary respite from the bitterness. "The court, I fear, has ventured into a minefield," Ginsburg had warned at the end of her *Hobby Lobby* dissent. Only three days after the final session, the first mine went off.

In *Hobby Lobby*, Alito had written for the majority that the government was required to offer for-profit businesses the same "accommodation" it had already offered religiously affiliated nonprofits. Under that arrangement, a religious nonprofit need only certify to the government that it objected to providing the insurance coverage for contraception; the government would then order the insurer to provide the coverage without additional charge to either the employer or the employee. (The rationale for shifting the cost was that women with access to contraception, over time, had fewer costs for childbirth and other health expenses than women without; thus providing the coverage would save the insurance companies money in the end.)

Hobby Lobby refused to say that this accommodation would satisfy it. Ginsburg noted that religious nonprofits were already in court challenging the "accommodation" (even filling out a form, they argued, made them complicit in an employee's contraceptive choices and thus violated RFRA). And, finally, the court itself had not actually held that the "accommodation" would resolve the religious-freedom issue.

On Thursday, July 3, the court suddenly issued an emergency order that seemed to confirm Ginsburg's fears. An evangelical Christian college, Wheaton, refused to fill out the form required to activate the "accommodation"; the court now blocked the government from requiring it to do so. This was a step beyond the emergency order issued by Sotomayor in December. The Little Sisters of the Poor, plaintiffs in the earlier case, were a "religious employer." Thus, even if the nuns signed the form, their employees would not receive contraceptive care because the statute provided their employer a complete exemption. Wheaton was a religious *nonprofit*, not a church or convent. The accommodation it was refusing was the one the court had suggested for Hobby Lobby.

The court took no note of this difference. If Wheaton objected to the form, the court's brief, unsigned opinion said that the government could simply rely on a letter from the college saying so. "Nothing in this interim order affects the ability of [Wheaton's] employees and students to obtain, without cost, the full range of FDA approved contraceptives," the brief order said. It added, "this order should not be construed as an expression of the court's views on the merits."

Legal observers were puzzled about how either statement could be correct. The order allowed Wheaton to submit a general letter instead of the form. Under regulations issued by the Department of HHS, the form itself was necessary before the agency could order the insurer to provide coverage. In fact, without the form, HHS might not even know who the college's insurance company was, and thus it could not order the company to provide the coverage. As Lyle Deniston of SCOTUSblog wrote, "There is nothing in existing government regulations that allows such a letter instead of the government form, and nothing in those regulations that says such a letter is enough to guarantee access to birth control. But the court order appears to be, in effect, a rewrite of those regulations." Rewriting administrative regulations is, as a general matter, not something courts have the authority to do.

And the emergency order itself, coming even before an adverse decision below, seemed like a fairly strong hint that a majority was prepared to strike down the "accommodation" it had acclaimed only a few days before. If the order was brief and unsigned, the accompanying dissent was neither. Justice Sonia Sotomayor wrote for all three of the female justices; in blistering language, she accused the majority of bad faith. Having dangled the "accommodation" before the government and the public, she implied, they had waited only days before snatching it away. "Those who are bound by our decisions usually believe they can take us at our word," she wrote. "Not so today. After expressly relying on the availability of the religious-nonprofit accommodation to hold that the contraceptive coverage requirement violates RFRA as applied to closely held for-profit corporations, the court now, as the dissent in *Hobby Lobby* feared it might, retreats from that position. That action evinces disregard for even the newest of this court's precedents and undermines confidence in this institution."

Legal commentators divided over whether the court's Thursday order was a retreat from the language in *Hobby Lobby*. The order was opaque; in fact, it was not even clear on its face which five justices had supported it. The three women dissented, meaning it could represent six at the most. Justice Scalia concurred only in the judgment, presumably wanting to invalidate the "accommodation" altogether. There was no notation where Justice Breyer had come down, but court scholars suggested that he must have voted with Roberts, Kennedy, Thomas, and Alito; otherwise, the order rewriting the regulations would not be the order "of the court."

Fine points of federal appellate practice, however, were not of much public interest as the Fourth of July holiday began. The nation had now heard from three justices themselves that the court's majority had lied.

News reports after the decision had speculated on which businesses would now come forward with demands for exemption from contraceptive coverage. "Closely held" corporations are not all small; indeed, by one estimate, more than half the American workforce is employed by them. It was not clear where a line would be drawn; what was obvious was that dozens of institutions would seek to be on the unregulated side of the line.

And, as Ginsburg had warned, the controversy was spreading to different areas. Already the day after the decision, officials of fourteen religious charities sent a letter to President Obama asking for a new kind of religious exemption. The charities provided various social services under contracts funded by the federal government. Obama had proposed rules banning government contractors from discriminating in employment against gays and lesbians. The signers included top officials of Catholic Charities USA, the Center for Public Justice, Gordon College, and Christianity Today. Many of these institutions refuse to hire or promote gays and lesbians, and the signers of the letter now urged Obama to allow them to continue discriminating while receiving federal funds.

"We must find a way to respect diversity of opinion on this issue in a way that respects the dignity of all parties to the best of our ability," the letter said. "There is no perfect solution that will make all parties perfectly happy." The groups' proposed solution was clothed in the language of compromise, but it was not a compromise. It imposed all costs on gay and lesbian employees. Unstated but implied was the threat that the companies would sue to block the new regulations and that the Supreme Court would again agree that the beliefs of religious employers must take precedence over the rights of their workers. After all, that was the rule in *Hobby Lobby* for contraception; why should it be different in the employment category?

There was certainly language in the *Hobby Lobby* opinion to encourage those hopes. Ginsburg's dissent questioned whether the new approach to religious exemption would permit employers to pay women less than men. Alito's response was revealing: "The government has a compelling interest in providing an equal opportunity to participate in the workforce without regard to *race*," he wrote, "and prohibitions on *racial discrimination* are precisely tailored to achieve that critical goal" (emphasis added). Ginsburg had written about discrimination against *women*. Alito pointedly did not concede that preventing sex discrimination was a "compelling" interest.

Thus *Hobby Lobby's* majority had thus refused even to affirm the national commitment to nondiscrimination based on sex. Would the five conservatives possibly believe government could override religious objections to hiring gays?

Less than a week after it left town, the court had found new fissures within itself. Worse yet, it was beginning to widen existing fissures in the country. As a result of *Hobby Lobby*, the nation would no longer simply be divided into red and blue states or red and blue districts; Americans would now work for red or blue companies.

In fact, it seemed, America now had red and blue justices on its highest court.

Hobby Lobby may have been about religious belief, but it was also very much about politics and partisanship. *Hobby Lobby* was a challenge to the ACA, Barack Obama's signature achievement. The act also represented a historic aim of the Obama's party. Democratic presidents since Harry Truman had sought to extend medical coverage to the nation as a whole; Republicans had bitterly fought this as "socialism."

In applying the RFRA broadly to the ACA, the *Hobby Lobby* majority had done just what it had done two years before. Without striking it down, it had weakened it, hollowed it out, and suggested that in some way it was less legitimate, less worthy of respect, than other laws. In 2012, the court had let stand the "individual mandate" but only as a tax, not (as scholars had expected) as a regulation of commerce; at the same time, it had allowed the expansion of Medicaid but empowered individual states to block this federal program. In 2014, it empowered individual employers to thwart national health policy and deprive women of health benefits the law said they had earned. Properly read, the opinion said that the contraceptive coverage mandate might—or might not—survive the next case; after the emergency *Wheaton College* order, it was hard not to suspect that the *Hobby Lobby* majority might, in fact, simply be setting that provision of the act up for a final knockout blow.

The ACA dispute had shut down the government in October. In July, as the court left town, it did so having made the dispute more, not less, bitter. It escaped no one that new challenges to the act were pending in lower courts. The court would again have a chance to fulfill Republican dreams of destroying the act. Would it do so? What would stop the five Republicans this time?

The Supreme Court had always been bipartisan, if not quite nonpartisan. In the earliest days, the Federalist John Marshall had been aided by the Republican Joseph Story. During the conservative ascendancy, Democratic judges like Louis D. Brandeis had made common cause with Republican progressives like Oliver Wendell Holmes and Charles Evans Hughes; Republican conservatives like William Howard Taft had found allies like former Democratic Attorney General James C. McReynolds. Earl Warren, symbol of the "liberal" court, had been a Republican politician; William Brennan, the leading liberal tactician of the Warren and Burger courts, had been a Republican state judge. The last three "liberals" to retire—Harry Blackmun, David Souter, and John Paul Stevens—had all been Republican appointees.

On the Roberts court, for perhaps the first time ever, the party identity of the justices seemed to be the single most important determinant of their votes. No Republican justice was consistently to the left of any Democrat or vice versa. Over the years, journalists and editors agonized about whether news accounts of court decisions should identify the judges by their party or by the name of the president who appointed them. After 2014, failing to do so might seem like journalistic malpractice.

The country as a whole had taken note. A poll taken immediately after the decision showed that 46 percent of the people approved of *Hobby Lobby*, while 41 percent disapproved. Seventy-seven percent of Republicans approved of the decision; 20 percent of Democrats did. Another poll taken before the last days of OT13 also showed that 60 percent of those polled disapproved of the current court, against only 33 percent who approved. The largest single complaint was that the court favored corporations and business interests over individual consumers and workers.

Supreme Court justices are insulated from polls, but sometimes they worry about issues of "legitimacy." In the autumn of 2005, John Roberts hoped to lead a court that would unite the nation and burnish the court's legitimacy. That wish now seemed as admirable and as vain as Barack Obama's hope that his election in 2008 would usher in a new era when Americans would not be divided by party and mutual suspicion.

For both men, as of June 2014, the fabric of this dream had melted into air, into thin air.

Appendix A

A Brief Guide to
Supreme Court Procedure

Even lawyers are confused about how the Supreme Court works and how cases get there. The system, which grew up without planning over two centuries, is intricate, based as much on tradition and inertia as planning or constitutional design. The court as an institution clings to its old ways—until the 1980s, each justice had a spittoon at his feet, even though the custom of chewing and spitting tobacco on the bench had passed out of fashion several generations earlier. Even today, the court honors lawyers who appear before it by presenting each with a quill pen, though handwritten briefs, however elegant, have not been accepted for well over a century.

In general outline, though, the system works this way. The Supreme Court convenes, by law, on the first Monday of October. This begins what is known as the "October term." The name is a legacy from the court's early days, when it conducted very little business. In 1801, the Federalists, defeated by the Jeffersonian Republicans, used their "lame duck" session to require two terms per year, one in June and one in December. The Republicans, who took power in 1801, hated the court and its new chief justice, John Marshall. In order to prevent Marshall's court from invalidating legislation, they abolished both the June and December terms of 1802, prescribing a single term to be convened in February 1803.

From then on, there has only been one term—it has begun on the first Monday of October since 1917—but the court's work has gradually expanded to fill the entire year. So Monday, October 7, 2013, began the "October 2013 term," which lasts until Sunday, October 4, 2014. All cases the court hears from October to October are then considered to be cases in "October Term 2013"; court insiders called it "OT13."

The court during OT13 would eventually hear and decide seventy cases. Since 1988, the court has had almost total control over its own docket. A few cases still come to the court on "appeal," meaning that Congress requires the court to decide them. But there are relatively few of them, now mostly consisting of decisions by three-judge courts applying the Voting Rights Act. Most cases, whether from the federal or state court systems, come to the court as "petitions for certiorari" (or, to court insiders, "cert.")—requests that the court reexamine a decision from a lower court.

OT13, like the previous recent terms, would bring as many as eight thousand petitions to the court from disappointed litigants around the country. The court did not need to hear most of them, but it did need to decide whether to hear them. That work alone consumed much of the efforts of the justices and their clerks, hardworking young law graduates who reviewed the petitions and recommend whether the court should "grant," bringing the case before the court, or "deny." Most of the justices have joined what is called the "cert. pool," in which all the clerks divide up the petitions. One clerk then carefully reads and researches each and prepares a memo that goes to all the member justices. Each justice reads the pool summary of all the cases and lets the chief justice know whether he or she wants to discuss the case at conference. The chief compiles a "discuss list" of cases to be discussed at a conference of the justices.

Cases make the "discuss list" because they present an issue or issues that one or more justices consider proper for the court's consideration. The Supreme Court today does not sit to correct mistakes made in courts below—even when those mistakes may result in unfairness to one of the parties. What lawyers call "error correction" is to be handled by the thirteen federal Courts of Appeals for federal cases and the state appellate courts for state disputes. What interests the Supreme Court are issues of national importance. This may mean simply that two different courts below have decided the same federal issue in opposite ways, so the court decides to step in and impose a uniform solution. It can also mean that questions have arisen about the proper reading of a federal statute that the court must resolve. Finally, it may mean that a question "arising under" the Constitution has to be tackled, even if it is a new one, because the nation needs an answer now.

Cases on the "discuss list" are considered at the court's hallowed conference, a procedure nearly as mysterious as the conclave of cardinals in the Vatican. Held in a conference room directly behind the court's bench at 1 First Street NE, it is attended only by justices. Not even a messenger may enter the room; if an emergency arises, a court employee will knock at the door while remaining respectfully outside. The junior justice must arise and go to the door to get the message.

Decisions about "discuss" cases are governed by the "rule of four"—if any four justices vote to hear a case, the court will "grant cert." and put the case down for argument. The first conference of the fall is held the week before the first Monday in October; it is called "the long conference" because the justices in former times might need all day to resolve the outstanding petitions. As chief justice, William Rehnquist streamlined procedure so that the "long conference" isn't very long. It may produce as many as a dozen grants of certiorari resulting from petitions that have been submitted in late spring and summer. From then on, the court will confer on the Friday before a two-week argument session and again on both Fridays of the session. The certiorari grants and other orders agreed on at a Friday conference are then announced the following Monday.

Not every "grant" means the court will hear the oral argument and write a full opinion. The court will often grant review in a case, vacate the judgment below, and remand, or send, the case back to the lower court. This is called a "GVR" ("grant, vacate, remand") and usually means that the court itself has made a decision that may change the result being appealed. The court may also take a case and summarily reverse or affirm the decision below, ending the litigation with no briefing or argument. Usually a brief opinion explains such a "summary" disposition—though not always. And sometimes, after certiorari has been granted, the court will discover that the case does *not* in fact present issues in a clear way and thus would not be a good vehicle for a full opinion of the court. These are "DIGS," cases in which certiorari is "dismissed as improvidently granted."

The few cases that survive the winnowing process get the full consideration of the court. That is a high-profile process in which the parties submit lengthy briefs and a voluminous record to point out the issues they want the justices to focus on. In an important case, there may also be dozens of "amicus briefs," from the expression "amicus curiae," or "friend of the court." (More specialized cases usually produce at least one or two "amici" on both sides.) These briefs come from individuals, trade associations, individual companies, state and local governments, think tanks, academic institutions, individual professors, or groups of professors, and nonprofit advocacy groups who want to let the court know how *they* think the justices should decide. These briefs may run to many thousands of pages in important cases, and justices take them seriously, often referring during oral argument or even in the final opinion to points raised by amici.

Oral argument is the final public step for a case granted full review. Oral argument takes place three days a week, two weeks a month, between October and April. Supreme Court argument is a dramatic and stylized form of legal combat. In most cases, each side receives thirty minutes. The "petitioner" (which usually means the loser below) argues first and may save up to five minutes for "rebuttal" after the "respondent" (usually the winner below) has argued for thirty minutes.

On rare occasions, the court will allow other parties to enter oral argument. Sometimes an "amicus," such as a group of members of Congress, may ask for a part of the time. On other occasions, when neither party is making an argument the court thinks important, it may appoint an amicus to argue that point.

Even when the federal government is not a party to a case, the issue may affect federal law; in that case, the court may seek the federal government's views. These are offered by the solicitor general of the United States, a figure who by statute must be "learned in the law." The "SG," as the holder is known, controls appellate litigation by all government agencies and determines the position the government will take in cases before the Supreme Court. It is a very significant job: one former SG, William Howard Taft, went on to become president and then chief justice; another, Charles Evans Hughes, was an associate justice, a Republican presidential nominee, and then chief justice. Four other former SGs have become justices, including current Justice Elena Kagan.

The presence of the SG's office at argument lends an air of anachronistic drama to important cases. By custom, the SG and lawyers from his office appear in "morning dress," long grey coats reminiscent of the Ascot Racecourse of Victorian England. (Kagan, the only female SG in history, refused to don "morning dress" and argued in ordinary business attire.)

In recent years, a small group of elite lawyers in major Washington law firms has emerged to dominate the arguments in front of the court. These lawyers know the justices well and vice versa, and the justices have confidence in their statements of fact and law. Sometimes they will volunteer to take on cases "pro bono" (or "for the public good") simply to gain the prestige and experience of another appearance before the court. They are remarkably quick on their feet and often argue a complicated case without a single note, even though they may have to refer to parts of a ten thousand–page record by page or even line number.

Argument may crackle with raw intelligence, surprising analysis, and even wit. At times, top lawyers feel relaxed enough to trade quips with the justices or even push up against the requirements of decorum. In 2012, former Solicitor General Seth Waxman, a favorite of the court, was arguing against a new federal rule that would punish television broadcasters for any displays of a "bare buttocks." Waxman looked up from the lectern and focused on the monumental frieze in the courtroom that depicts lawgivers from history and myth: "Right over here, Justice Scalia," he said, pointing up and to his right. "There's a bare buttock here and a bare buttock there," he continued. "There may be more that I hadn't seen. But frankly, I had never focused on it before. But the point . . ."

Justice Scalia interrupted, "I hadn't either," and the moment passed in laughter.

Few indeed, however, are the advocates who can take such liberties with the decorum of the courtroom. (That same case concerned indecent language as well as images, and according to news reports, the chief justice had sent word to the lawyers that they were not to use the forbidden words in his courtroom.) And woe betide the lawyer unknown to or disliked by the justices who steps over the line.

Beyond the SG and the top private lawyers, other "frequent filers" are major state attorneys general and advocacy organizations like the National Right to Work Legal

Defense Foundation, the American Civil Liberties Union, and the National Association for the Advancement of Colored People Legal Defense and Education Fund. But scattered in this roster of prominent barristers, each two-week sitting usually presents the spectacle of a state public defender, a small-town lawyer, or a state attorney general seizing a once-in-a-lifetime chance to argue from the hallowed well of the court.

Despite the court's motto, "equal justice under law," such inexperienced lawyers seldom do well. Indeed, not only are their clients ill served, but the lawyers themselves often experience personal humiliation as the justices vent their frustration at a lawyer's inability to answer important questions about his or her own case. During the 2013 term alone, Justice Scalia berated one lawyer for briefing his case so poorly that the court had to DIG it and humiliated another for reading too closely from his notes. "Counsel, you are not reading this, are you?" Scalia said, producing a seemingly endless five-second silence until Justice Breyer rescued him by saying, "It's all right." (This inept advocate, in the end, won his case.)

After oral argument—on Wednesday afternoons and Friday mornings—the justices gather in conference to vote on the cases they have heard. Though votes are taken then, within a few days, it may be months before the country will learn the result. If the chief justice has agreed with the result, it is his prerogative to assign the majority opinion to the justice of his choice; if he is in the minority, then the senior justice in the majority, the one who has served longest, has that prerogative. The justice with the assignment prepares an opinion—which can range in length between a dozen and a hundred pages, depending on the complexity of the issue. Meanwhile, those in opposition decide which of them will write the principal dissent; again, selecting the dissent's author is the prerogative of the senior dissenting justice. Drafts of both must be circulated to each justice, who can offer suggestions for changes. Sometimes disagreements break out at this stage; in fact, it has sometimes happened that a majority opinion has "lost the court," meaning that one or two justices, unpersuaded, have switched their votes and reversed the result. Sometimes the switcher is the justice assigned to write the majority opinion; he or she may find that the opinion "won't write."

Other justices, of course, are free to write separate opinions as well, specifying parts of the other opinions with which they agree or disagree. All must be circulated in multiple drafts. Sometimes there is no one opinion that commands a majority. Such cases are said to be decided by a plurality, and they pose a question for the lawyer or reporter trying to figure out how the case has changed the law. This task is made even more complicated because justices may join a plurality opinion only in part, specifically disclaiming one section or even one footnote. Here is an important example, placed at the beginning of *National Federation of Independent Business v. Sebelius*, the wrenching 2012 decision upholding part but not all of the ACA:

> ROBERTS, C. J., announced the judgment of the court and delivered the opinion of the court with respect to Parts I, II, and III-C, in which GINSBURG, BREYER, SOTOMAYOR, and KAGAN, JJ., joined; an opinion with respect to Part IV, in which BREYER and KAGAN, JJ., joined; and an opinion with respect

to Parts III-A, III-B, and III-D. GINSBURG, J., filed an opinion concurring in part, concurring in the judgment in part, and dissenting in part, in which SOTOMAYOR, J., joined, and in which BREYER and KAGAN, JJ., joined as to Parts I, II, III, and IV. SCALIA, KENNEDY, THOMAS, and ALITO, JJ., filed a dissenting opinion. THOMAS, J., filed a dissenting opinion.

Even experienced lawyers sometimes are stymied when the court speaks in many voices. In 1977, the court itself furnished a guide to interpreting a plurality decision. In a case called *Marks v. United States*, a majority wrote that "when a fragmented court decides a case and no single rationale explaining the result enjoys the assent of five justices, the holding of the court may be viewed as that position taken by those Members who concurred in the judgments on the narrowest grounds." Thus, for example, if four justices think a statute is completely unconstitutional but a fifth thinks it is constitutional but simply should not apply to the case in front of the court, the case would stand for the view of that one justice. A decision by one or even a few justices will have less precedential force than a decision by a majority. Lower courts may disagree on what that justice actually meant, but they are not free (as some state court judges have claimed) to ignore the opinion.

Most justices say they try to avoid those split decisions. Those on the inside of the court insist that very little "horse trading" or lobbying for votes goes on between the justices. A specific justice with an assignment, however, may seek to craft an opinion so that five or more will join; if one justice threatens to write a separate opinion, the assigned justice may try to revise his or her opinion to satisfy the wavering justice. Sometimes this is accomplished by making the language of a decision deliberately opaque or ambiguous, postponing thorny issues for later cases. This process of negotiating opinions is carried on in a blizzard of draft opinions and accompanying memos, and it can be time consuming. The justices, by all accounts, do very little one-on-one conferring or negotiating; the Supreme Court runs on paper.

The decision in an argued case is announced from the bench during a regular session of the court. If an opinion is ready for release, the session begins with the chief justice's announcement, "Justice X has our opinion in case number Y." The justice writing the opinion of the court will then read an oral summary of the opinion. He or she will then announce the lineup of justices: if any justice has written a separate concurrence or a dissent, the first justice will announce the names of the concurring or dissenting justices.

Sometimes the dissenting justice will read an oral summary of the dissent. (In *Bond v. United States*, for the first time in the history of the Court, one justice, Scalia, read aloud his *concurrence* in a case. The concurrence was so vitriolic, however, that it seemed like a dissent.) Such moments are becoming more common but can still be quite dramatic. They are seen as a direct challenge to the majority opinion and its author and sometimes leave scars. The most famous example occurred in 1961, when Chief Justice Earl Warren berated Justice Felix Frankfurter in open court for the tone of a dissent from the bench: "As I understand it," the chief said to a shocked audience, "the purpose of reporting an opinion in the courtroom is to inform the public and is not for the purpose of degrading this court." Usually, however, the façade of politeness is maintained even when the dissent reveals sharp division on the court.

Announcement of opinions begins as soon as one is approved; some may be announced within a few weeks of oral argument. The first full opinion of OT13 was announced on November 5, resolving a case argued October 8. But preparation of the more complex and divisive opinions can be time-consuming. After April, the court ordinarily hears no more arguments. Sessions continue throughout May and June for the purpose of announcing opinions as they are ready. The parties and lawyers to a case are rarely in the courtroom when their cases are announced; the court gives no hint to the public of which case will be announced when.

It is very rare for the court to hold sessions after the end of June. At the last session, the chief justice declares, "The court will be in recess from today until the first Monday in October [of the current year], at which time the October Term of the court [of the past year] will be adjourned and the October term [of the current year] will begin as provided by law."

With that announcement, the justices vanish behind the curtain and, usually, head out of town shortly thereafter. Barring an emergency, they will not gather again until the "long conference" in the fall.

Appendix B

Biographies of Current Justices of the Supreme Court

All biographies are derived from the US Supreme Court website: http://www.supremecourt.gov/biographies.aspx.

Chief Justice

John G. Roberts Jr., chief justice of the United States, was born in Buffalo, New York, January 27, 1955. He married Jane Marie Sullivan in 1996 and they have two children—Josephine and John. He received an AB from Harvard College in 1976 and a JD from Harvard Law School in 1979. He served as a law clerk for Judge Henry J. Friendly of the US Court of Appeals for the Second Circuit from 1979 to 1980 and as a law clerk for then Associate Justice William H. Rehnquist of the US Supreme Court during the 1980 term. He was special assistant to the attorney general, US Department of Justice, from 1981 to 1982; associate counsel to President Ronald Reagan, White

House Counsel's Office, from 1982 to 1986; and principal deputy solicitor general, US Department of Justice, from 1989 to 1993. From 1986 to 1989 and 1993 to 2003, he practiced law in Washington, DC. He was appointed to the US Court of Appeals for the DC Circuit in 2003. President George W. Bush nominated him as chief justice of the United States, and he took his seat September 29, 2005.

Associate Justices

All justices are listed in descending order of seniority.

Antonin Scalia was born in Trenton, New Jersey, on March 11, 1936. He married Maureen McCarthy and has nine children—Ann Forrest, Eugene, John Francis, Catherine Elisabeth, Mary Clare, Paul David, Matthew, Christopher James, and Margaret Jane. He received his AB from Georgetown University and the University of Fribourg, Switzerland; received his LLB from Harvard Law School; and was a Sheldon Fellow of Harvard University from 1960 to 1961. He was in private practice in Cleveland, Ohio, from 1961 to 1967; a professor of law at the University of Virginia from 1967 to 1971; a professor of law at the University of Chicago from 1977 to 1982; and a visiting professor of law at Georgetown University and Stanford University. He was chairman of the American Bar Association's Section of Administrative Law, 1981–82, and its Conference of Section Chairmen, 1982–1983. He served the federal government as general counsel for the Office of Telecommunications Policy from 1971 to 1972, chairman of the Administrative Conference of the United States from 1972 to 1974, and assistant attorney general for the Office of Legal Counsel from 1974 to 1977. He was appointed judge of the US Court of Appeals for the DC Circuit in 1982. President Ronald Reagan nominated him as an associate justice of the Supreme Court, and he took his seat September 26, 1986.

Anthony M. Kennedy was born in Sacramento, California, July 23, 1936. He married Mary Davis and has three children. He received his BA from Stanford University and the London School of Economics, and his LLB from Harvard Law School. He was in private practice in San Francisco, California, from 1961 to 1963, as well as in Sacramento, California, from 1963 to 1975. From 1965 to 1988, he was a professor of constitutional law at the McGeorge School of Law, University of the Pacific. He has served in numerous positions during his career, including as a member of the California Army National Guard in 1961, the board of the Federal Judicial Center from 1987 to 1988, and two committees of the Judicial Conference of the United States: the Advisory Panel on Financial Disclosure Reports and Judicial Activities, subsequently renamed the Advisory Committee on Codes of Conduct, from 1979 to 1987, and the Committee on Pacific Territories from 1979 to 1990, which he chaired from 1982 to 1990. He was appointed to the US Court of Appeals for the Ninth Circuit in 1975. President Ronald Reagan nominated him as an associate justice of the Supreme Court, and he took his seat February 18, 1988.

Clarence Thomas was born in the Pin Point community of Georgia near Savannah June 23, 1948. He married Virginia Lamp in 1987 and has one child, Jamal Adeen, by a previous marriage. He attended Conception Seminary and received an AB cum laude from Holy Cross College and a JD from Yale Law School in 1974. He was admitted to law practice in Missouri in 1974 and served as an assistant attorney general of Missouri from 1974 to 1977, an attorney with the Monsanto Company from 1977 to 1979, and legislative assistant to Senator John Danforth from 1979 to 1981. From 1981 to 1982, he served as assistant secretary for civil rights, US Department of Education, and as chairman of the US Equal Employment Opportunity Commission from 1982 to 1990. He became a judge of the US Court of Appeals for the DC Circuit in 1990. President George H. W. Bush nominated him as an associate justice of the Supreme Court, and he took his seat October 23, 1991.

Ruth Bader Ginsburg was born in Brooklyn, New York, March 15, 1933. She married Martin D. Ginsburg in 1954, and has a daughter, Jane, and a son, James. She received her BA from Cornell University, attended Harvard Law School, and received her LLB from Columbia Law School. She served as a law clerk to the Honorable Edmund L. Palmieri, judge of the US District Court for the Southern District of New York, from 1959 to 1961. From 1961 to 1963, she was a research associate and then associate director of the Columbia Law School Project on International Procedure. She was a professor of law at Rutgers University School of Law from 1963 to 1972 and Columbia Law School from 1972 to 1980 and a fellow at the Center for Advanced Study in the Behavioral Sciences in Stanford, California, from 1977 to 1978. In 1971, she was cofounder of the Women's Rights Project of the American Civil Liberties Union and served as the ACLU's general counsel from 1973 to 1980 and on the ACLU National Board of

Directors from 1974 to 1980. She served on the Board and Executive Committee of the American Bar Foundation from 1979 to 1989, on the Board of Editors of the *American Bar Association Journal* from 1972 to 1978, and on the Council of the American Law Institute from 1978 to 1993. She was appointed a judge of the US Court of Appeals for the DC Circuit in 1980. President William Clinton nominated her as an associate justice of the Supreme Court, and she took her seat August 10, 1993.

Stephen G. Breyer was born in San Francisco, California, August 15, 1938. He married Joanna Hare in 1967, and has three children—Chloe, Nell, and Michael. He received an AB from Stanford University; a BA from Magdalen College, Oxford; and an LLB from Harvard Law School. He served as a law clerk to Justice Arthur Goldberg of the US Supreme Court during the 1964 term; as a special assistant to the assistant US attorney general for antitrust, 1965–67; as an assistant special prosecutor of the Watergate Special Prosecution Force, 1973; as special counsel of the US Senate Judiciary Committee, 1974–75; and as chief counsel of the committee, 1979–80. He was an assistant professor, professor of law, and lecturer at Harvard Law School, 1967–94; a professor at the Harvard University Kennedy School of Government, 1977–80; and a visiting professor at the College of Law, Sydney, Australia, and at the University of Rome. From 1980 to 1990, he served as a judge of the US Court of Appeals for the First Circuit and as its chief judge, 1990–94. He also served as a member of the Judicial Conference of the United States, 1990–94, and the US Sentencing Commission, 1985–89. President William Clinton nominated him as an associate justice of the Supreme Court, and he took his seat August 3, 1994.

Samuel Anthony Alito Jr. was born in Trenton, New Jersey, April 1, 1950. He married Martha-Ann Bomgardner in 1985, and has two children—Philip and Laura. He served as a law clerk for Leonard I. Garth of the US Court of Appeals for the Third Circuit from 1976 to 1977. He was assistant US attorney, District of New Jersey, 1977–81; assistant to the solicitor general, US Department of Justice, 1981–85; deputy assistant attorney general, US Department of Justice, 1985–87; and US attorney, District of New Jersey, 1987–90. He was appointed to the US Court of Appeals for the Third Circuit in 1990. President George W. Bush nominated him as an associate justice of the Supreme Court, and he took his seat January 31, 2006.

Sonia Sotomayor was born in Bronx, New York, on June 25, 1954. She earned a BA in 1976 from Princeton University, graduating summa cum laude and receiving the university's highest academic honor. In 1979, she earned a JD from Yale Law School, where she served as an editor of the *Yale Law Journal.* She served as assistant district attorney in the New York County District Attorney's Office from 1979 to 1984. She then litigated international commercial matters in New York City at Pavia and Harcourt, where she served as an associate and then partner from 1984 to 1992. In 1991, President George H. W. Bush nominated her to the US District Court, Southern District of New York, and she served in that role from 1992 to 1998. She served as a judge on the US Court of Appeals for the Second Circuit from 1998 to 2009. President Barack

Obama nominated her as an associate justice of the Supreme Court on May 26, 2009, and she assumed this role August 8, 2009.

Elena Kagan was born in New York, New York, on April 28, 1960. She received an AB from Princeton in 1981, an M Phil from Oxford in 1983, and a JD from Harvard Law School in 1986. She clerked for Judge Abner Mikva of the US Court of Appeals for the DC Circuit from 1986 to 1987 and for Justice Thurgood Marshall of the US Supreme Court during the 1987 term. After briefly practicing law at a Washington, DC, law firm, she became a law professor, first at the University of Chicago Law School and later at Harvard Law School. She also served for four years in the Clinton Administration as associate counsel to the president and then as deputy assistant to the president for domestic policy. Between 2003 and 2009, she served as the dean of Harvard Law School. In 2009, President Barack Obama nominated her as the solicitor general of the United States. After serving in that role for a year, the president nominated her as an associate justice of the Supreme Court on May 10, 2010. She took her seat August 7, 2010.

Retired Justices

All justices are listed in order of retirement.

Sandra Day O'Connor, (retired) associate justice, was born in El Paso, Texas, March 26, 1930. She married John Jay O'Connor III in 1952 and has three sons—Scott, Brian, and Jay. She received her BA and LLB from Stanford University. She served as Deputy County Attorney of San Mateo County, California, from 1952 to 1953 and as a civilian attorney for Quartermaster Market Center, Frankfurt, Germany, from 1954 to 1957. From 1958 to 1960, she practiced law in Maryvale, Arizona, and served as assistant attorney general of Arizona from 1965 to 1969. She was appointed to the Arizona State Senate in 1969 and was subsequently reelected to two two-year terms. In 1975 she was elected judge of the Maricopa County Superior Court and served until 1979, when she was appointed to the Arizona Court of Appeals. President Ronald Reagan nominated her as an associate justice of the Supreme Court, and she took her seat September 25, 1981. Justice O'Connor retired from the Supreme Court on January 31, 2006.

David H. Souter, (retired) associate justice, was born in Melrose, Massachusetts, September 17, 1939. He graduated from Harvard College, from which he received his AB. After two years as a Rhodes Scholar at Magdalen College, Oxford, he received an AB in Jurisprudence from Oxford University and an MA in 1989. After receiving an LLB from Harvard Law School, he was an associate at Orr and Reno in Concord, New Hampshire, from 1966 to 1968, when he became an assistant attorney general of New Hampshire. In 1971, he became deputy attorney general and, in 1976, attorney general of New Hampshire. In 1978, he was named an associate justice of the Superior Court of New Hampshire and was appointed to the Supreme Court of New Hampshire as an associate justice in 1983. He became a judge of the US Court of Appeals for the First Circuit on May 25, 1990. President George

H. W. Bush nominated him as an associate justice of the Supreme Court, and he took his seat October 9, 1990. Justice Souter retired from the Supreme Court on June 29, 2009.

John Paul Stevens, (retired) associate justice, was born in Chicago, Illinois, April 20, 1920. He married Maryan Mulholland and has four children—John Joseph (deceased), Kathryn, Elizabeth Jane, and Susan Roberta. He received an AB from the University of Chicago and a JD from the Northwestern University School of Law. He served in the US Navy from 1942 to 1945 and was a law clerk to Justice Wiley Rutledge of the US Supreme Court during the 1947 term. He was admitted to law practice in Illinois in 1949. He was associate counsel to the Subcommittee on the Study of Monopoly Power of the Judiciary Committee of the US House of Representatives, 1951–52, and a member of the attorney general's National Committee to Study Antitrust Law, 1953–55. He was second vice president of the Chicago Bar Association in 1970. From 1970 to 1975, he served as a judge of the US Court of Appeals for the Seventh Circuit. President Gerald Ford nominated him as an associate justice of the Supreme Court, and he took his seat December 19, 1975. Justice Stevens retired from the Supreme Court on June 29, 2010.

Appendix C

Major OT13 Cases Discussed in This Book

Bond v. United States—The court decided unanimously that the government could not use the Chemical Warfare Convention Implementation Act of 1998 to prosecute a defendant in Pennsylvania who smeared toxic chemicals on the mailbox of a romantic rival. Four justices would have invalidated the act as beyond the treaty power. November 5, 2013–June 2, 2014. Opinion: Roberts. Concurrences: Scalia, Thomas, Alito.

Burwell v. Hobby Lobby Stores—By a 5–4 margin, the court decided that a for-profit corporation has rights to "the free exercise of religion" under the Religious Freedom Restoration Act and thus can refuse to follow provisions of the ACA requiring its health plan to cover the full range of medically approved contraceptive devices. March 25, 2014–June 30, 2014. Opinion: Alito. Concurrence: Kennedy. Dissent: Ginsburg.

Hall v. Florida—By a 5–4 margin, the court held that states may not set a rigid IQ cutoff for defendants who qualify as "intellectually disabled" and are thus ineligible for the death penalty. March 3, 2014–May 27, 2014. Opinion: Kennedy. Dissents: Scalia, Alito.

Harris v. Quinn—By a 5–4 margin, the court held that a contract requiring home health-care workers paid by the state of Illinois to contribute "agency fees" to a public-employee union violated the First Amendment. January 21, 2014–June 30, 2014. Opinion: Alito; Dissent: Kagan.

McCullen v. Coakley—The court unanimously decided that a state statute prescribing a thirty-five-foot "buffer zone" around abortion facilities violated the First Amendment rights to speech and assembly. The justices split 5–4 on the reasoning. January 15, 2014–June 26, 2014. Opinion: Roberts. Concurrences: Scalia, Alito.

McCutcheon v. Federal Election Commission—By a 5–4 margin, the court invalidated limits on the total amount an individual can contribute to all candidates during any one federal election cycle. October 8, 2013–April 2, 2014. Opinion: Roberts. Dissent: Breyer.

National Labor Relations Board v. Noel Canning—The court unanimously decided that the president may not make "recess appointments" under Article II, § 3 of the Constitution ("to fill up all vacancies that may happen during the recess of the Senate") when the Senate remains in pro forma session, meeting every three days but not transacting business. The justices split 5–4 on the reasoning. January 13, 2014–June 26, 2014. Majority: Breyer; Concurrence: Scalia.

Riley v. California—The court decided unanimously that police need a warrant to search the contents of a cell phone found on the person of an individual after a lawful arrest. April 29, 2014–June 25, 2014. Opinion: Roberts. Concurrence: Alito.

Schuette v. Coalition to Defend Affirmative Action by Any Means Necessary—By a 6–2 margin, the court approved a Michigan referendum outlawing any use of race- or gender-based affirmative action in state college and university admissions. October 15, 2013–April 22, 2014. Opinion: Kennedy. Concurrences: Scalia, Breyer. Dissent: Sotomayor. Recused: Kagan.

Susan B. Anthony List v. Driehaus—The court unanimously decided that a political action group could sue to set aside a state law barring "any person" from making false statements about candidates in state and federal elections during a political campaign. April 22, 2014–June 16, 2014. Opinion: Thomas.

Town of Greece v. Galloway—By a 5–4 margin, the court approved a town council's use of explicitly Christian prayers to begin its public meetings. November 6, 2013–May 5, 2013. Opinion: Kennedy. Concurrences: Thomas, Alito. Dissent: Kagan.

Further Reading

The Supreme Court Generally

Linda Greenhouse, *The Supreme Court: A Very Short Introduction by Linda Greenhouse* (Oxford, 2012). A general overview of the institution by the Pulitzer Prize–winning *New York Times* columnist and correspondent.

William H. Rehnquist, *The Supreme Court* (Random House, 2nd ed., 2001). The late chief justice readably explains his view of the court's history.

The Roberts Court

Joan Biskupic, *Breaking In: The Rise of Sonia Sotomayor and the Politics of Justice* (Crichton Books, forthcoming). The definitive account of the evolution of Sotomayor from novice jurist to "the people's justice."

Marcia Coyle, *The Roberts Court* (Simon and Schuster, 2013). An even-handed, thorough examination of the court, from Roberts's appointment until the Affordable Care Act decisions in 2012, by a longtime reporter for *National Law Journal*.

Further Reading

Jan Crawford Greenburg, *Supreme Conflict: The Inside Story of the Struggle for Control of the United States Supreme Court* (Penguin, 2007). A veteran television correspondent reviews the transition from Rehnquist to Roberts.

Jeffrey Toobin, *The Nine: Inside the Secret World of the Supreme Court* (Anchor, 2007), and *The Oath: The Obama White House and the Supreme Court* (Anchor, 2012). An account of the transition from the Rehnquist to the Roberts court, with a sequel examining the years between the 2009 inauguration of Barack Obama and the Affordable Care Act decision, by the CNN correspondent and *New Yorker* columnist.

By the Justices

Stephen Breyer, *Active Liberty: Interpreting Our Democratic Constitution* (Knopf, 2005), and *Making Our Democracy Work: A Judge's View* (Knopf, 2010). The justice's own explanation of his pragmatic philosophy of judicial review.

Antonin Scalia, *A Matter of Interpretation: Federal Courts and the Law* (Princeton, 1998). An extended essay by Scalia on "originalism" and legal interpretation, with short responses by prominent scholars.

Sonia Sotomayor, *My Beloved World* (Knopf, 2013). A vivid memoir of the justice's rise from Puerto Rican life in Bronx housing projects to a seat on the Supreme Court.

Clarence Thomas, *My Grandfather's Son* (HarperCollins, 2007). A haunting memoir of the justice's childhood in the segregated South and the later emergence of his conservative philosophy.

Useful Websites

http://www.supremecourt.gov. The court's official website offers latest opinions and orders, a comprehensive calendar of the current term, and audio and written transcripts of oral arguments.

http://www.scotusblog.com. Operated by the private firm of Goldstein and Russell, PC, this is an indispensable source of documentation

and commentary on the court, featuring live-blogging of opinions and orders, near-instantaneous reporting of arguments
and decisions, and detailed analyses before and after decisions
by the most prominent scholars and lawyers studying the court.
SCOTUSblog chief correspondent Lyle Deniston has covered the
court for more than half a century.

CPSIA information can be obtained at www.ICGtesting.com
Printed in the USA
BVOW01*1955260814

364353BV00002B/3/P